Drops in the Ocean

Peter Gill

Drops in the ocean
The work of Oxfam 1960-1970

Macdonald Unit 75 · London

First published in Great Britain in 1970 by
Macdonald Unit 75
St Giles House, 49/50 Poland Street,
London, W.1

Hardback SBN 356 03568 9
Paperback SBN 356 03584 0

Made and printed in Great Britain by
Hazell Watson & Viney Ltd
Aylesbury, Bucks

Photographs by Peter Gill, Tom Hanley, Tony Morrison,
Barney Wood, and Oxfam
Cover illustration by Derick Garnier
Cover design by Alwyn Timms

Contents

Preface

Before I started work on this book, my views on Oxfam coincided with those generally expressed by the sceptical. I doubted whether the money was effectively spent, hinted at abuses, and suspected that administrative costs were too high. Now that I have finished, I am not exactly a convert. Oxfam looks not for 'converts', but for those who appreciate the nature of world poverty and act. Nor was my tour of Oxfam projects drawn up to show me just the successes; it aimed rather at giving me a general insight into Oxfam's work. And for the record, Oxfam has approved my text only in the sense of correcting errors, and has suppressed neither uncomfortable facts nor disquieting opinions. The most pertinent criticism of Oxfam's work came, I found, from members of its own staff.

My thanks are due to those who welcomed and helped me on my tour. To some of Oxfam's representatives in the field I owe a special debt, but I also received much assistance from government officials, from the staff of United Nations agencies, and from the organisers of individual projects which Oxfam has aided. Next I must thank the younger members of Oxfam of Canada, in Toronto, who emphasised to me the wider implications of our relationship with the developing world, and Antony Tasker, director of the Overseas Development Institute, in London, who gave me further and valuable insights into the issue. I would also thank Oxfam's staff at home, and in particular Elizabeth Stamp, Oxfam's Information Officer, whose prompt answer to my many queries has been rivalled only by her generous encouragement while I have been writing the book.

Over the past few months I have said to many of these people that I hoped I could do justice to their work in print. It was, perhaps, a forlorn hope. But should any of them consider I have done so, they may regard this book as dedicated to their continued efforts.

Introduction

The years 1960 to 1970 comprised, for those of us who need a reminder, the Development Decade. Declared as such by the United Nations, it would have been no more than a pious aspiration had not the UN Food and Agriculture Organisation launched their Freedom from Hunger Campaign in 1961. 'Give a man a fish,' they said, 'and you feed him for a day; teach him to fish and you feed him for a life-time.' Relief work, of course, keeps the hungry alive. But a larger purpose would be served if international organisations, governments and private agencies would work to alleviate the effects of erratic rainfall, poor soil, and harsh climates.

For Oxfam there was an element of old hat in these arguments. It dates its first development project in 1947 when a group of Protestant churchmen in Germany was given money to establish a technical training centre for destitute young refugees from the East. Nevertheless it was the Freedom from Hunger Campaign, and the interest it generated in the United Kingdom, that launched Oxfam on its own development decade.

In the first year of the campaign Oxfam committed £500,000 to FFHC projects, a sum that was reviewed in 1963. A further £1,800,000 was pledged that year, and later transferred to the field. Oxfam did more than that. It decided to concentrate its efforts in the three British Protectorates of Bechuanaland, Basutoland, and Swaziland in southern Africa. To these ends it sent Jimmy Betts to prepare a survey of the needs of the territories and subsequently appointed him their first Field Director to supervise the programme, costing £500,000, which emerged from his survey. At that time, when African Colonies were winning their independence, the British Government liked to refer to these territories as a 'shop window for the Commonwealth'. The Government and Oxfam

9

Total Income and Components

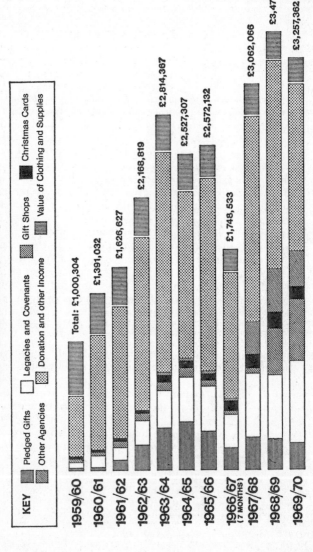

KEY

Pledged Gifts | Legacies and Covenants | Gift Shops | Christmas Cards
Other Agencies | Donation and other Income | Value of Clothing and Supplies

1959/60 — Total: £1,000,304
1960/61 — £1,391,032
1961/62 — £1,626,627
1962/63 — £2,168,819
1963/64 — £2,814,367
1964/65 — £2,527,307
1965/66 — £2,572,132
1966/67 (7 MONTHS) — £1,748,533
1967/68 — £3,062,066
1968/69 — £3,471,575
1969/70 — £3,257,362

are still heavily committed there. Bechuanaland, now independent Botswana, formed part of my tour for Oxfam. Much remains to be done before it achieves the status of a showplace.

On 9 July 1960, Richard Dimbleby gave the Week's Good Cause Appeal on behalf of Oxfam. Apart from raising a record sum of £105,941, Dimbleby described Oxfam as 'a sort of financial fire brigade, always ready, day and night, to send immediate help to any danger point, to any disaster in the world'. That, perhaps, was the reality then, and it remains Oxfam's image to this day. The reality, however, has changed. Of the £2,062,525 which went overseas in cash grants in 1969–70, only £161,783 was spent during emergencies and on feeding programmes. More than half of the total (£1,088,172) was spent on improving medical facilities and on other welfare projects in areas which had suffered no disaster. And as much as £809,056 was devoted exclusively to agricultural development and to technical training.

This is not to say that Oxfam has lost interest in helping in disasters. On the contrary, the £589,000 which was sent in emergency grants in 1968–9 represented the largest ever annual allocation for such a purpose. What it does mean is that Oxfam's income has grown sufficiently during the decade to enable it to spend far more on development work – on providing equipment and material for hospitals, clinics, technical schools and agricultural programmes – while maintaining its reputation for quick and effective help in emergencies. Of these there has been no shortage in the sixties.

The development decade opened with war in the Congo and closed with war in Nigeria. In between there were wars in India and the still unresolved horrors of Vietnam and the Middle East. Oxfam has been closely associated with relief work in all these situations. Indeed the organisation's largest single grant of the decade was of £150,000 towards providing food for Palestinian refugees in Jordan and Gaza.

As well as suffering and homelessness provoked by man, there has also been a dreadful harvest of natural disaster. Private aid organisations like Oxfam are invariably the quickest to act after floods, cyclones, hurricanes, and earthquakes. This year – the opening of the UN's second development decade – has already had a cruelly large share of such

11

disasters. A few weeks before I set off to look at Oxfam's work in the field, an earthquake hit western Turkey. My tour was only a week or so old when the Danube and its tributaries burst their banks to inundate all but two of 39 districts in Rumania. And in the heat of northern Ghana as I looked forward to inspecting Radio Schools in the cool of the Andes, I learnt of an earthquake in Peru that had killed upwards of 30,000 and destroyed 80,000 houses.

A shift of emphasis from relief to development work is not the only change that has overcome Oxfam in the last decade. It now strikes me as an organisation properly geared both to tapping the sources of public generosity in this country and to assessing the needs of the developing world. In its first annual report of the sixties, Oxfam announced the opening of an office in London to provide representation in the capital, and the establishment of a regional office in Leeds to serve Yorkshire. There are now 29 full-time regional organisers who work in conjunction with countless local groups and committees. In Oxford, too, the organisation now has a headquarters that is more in step with the need to despatch business rapidly. Before Oxfam House was built in 1962, the director worked over a tailor's shop, his deputy's office was on the other side of the road, committee meetings were held in the back room of a Baptist church, and the card index was kept in a condemned shed on loan from Oxford City Council.

It is, however, Oxfam's Field Directorate, its overseas arm, that is the envy of many other organisations – including, let it be said, at least one former British Minister of Overseas Development. Jimmy Betts's mission to southern Africa in 1961 led to his appointment there as Oxfam Field Director. When he moved to Nairobi in 1964 and a new Field Director took over in the south, his empire extended nearly the whole way from the Cape to Cairo encompassing both East Africa and Ethiopia. In 1964 Bernard Llewellyn, who now acts as the sometimes harsh appraiser of Oxfam's overseas aid programme, became Field Director in the Far East. And Jim Howard, a sturdy and forceful Quaker who had worked on an agricultural project in the Indian State of Madhya Pradesh, was recruited to cover that entire sub-continent.

By 1965 Oxfam had five Field Directors, three in Africa, one in India, and one in the Far East. There are now double that

The types of aid which Oxfam gives comparing 1960 with 1970

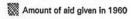

▨ Amount of aid given in 1960

█ Amount of aid given in 1970

Relief Aid

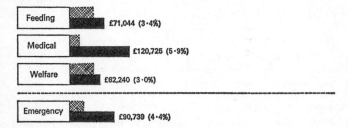

Feeding — £71,044 (3·4%)

Medical — £120,725 (5·9%)

Welfare — £62,240 (3·0%)

Emergency — £90,739 (4·4%)

Development Aid

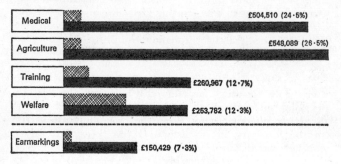

Medical — £504,510 (24·5%)

Agriculture — £548,089 (26·5%)

Training — £260,967 (12·7%)

Welfare — £253,782 (12·3%)

Earmarkings — £150,429 (7·3%)

number, with three in India, one in the Far East, four in Africa, one in the Middle East, and two in South America. The latest recruit is Charles Skinner, who, from Peru, covers all the Andean countries. There can be few Englishmen with a wider experience of South America. He has worked for the Bank of London and South America in Peru and Chile, for an American mining company all over the Andes, and as First Secretary in our Embassies in Brasilia and Lima.

As Oxfam's staff in the developing world has grown during the decade, so too has an interest in Oxfam's work in the developed world. In 1960 its fund-raising activities were confined to the United Kingdom. Now there is an Oxfam of Canada, an Oxfam Belgique, and an Oxfam America is on the drawing board. Of these sister organisations, Oxfam of Canada is the largest. In 1966, the year in which it was incorporated under a federal charter, it raised a little over £20,000. In the past four years, owing largely to sponsored walks, its income has increased twenty-fold. Last year it raised more than £600,000. And Oxfam Belgique reached the £30,000 mark for the first time during the past year.

No country other than Canada and Belgium yet has an Oxfam organisation of its own. But there are fund-raising groups in Denmark, Gibraltar, Italy, the Bahamas, and elsewhere, and supporters in countries from Hong Kong to Argentina. Two such groups in the Bahamas have raised more than £9,000 in the past year. During the Christmas period one island contributed the equivalent of 1s. 10d. per head. Had that figure been reflected throughout the United Kingdom last Christmas, Oxfam would have raised over £8 million. It was not.

Nevertheless it is Oxfam's dramatic and sustained growth over the decade which has allowed it to assume the role of a development agency. In the first complete financial year of the sixties, the organisation broke the £1 million cash barrier for the first time in its history. Of the £1,000,304 raised, £876,408 was disbursed in overseas grants during the year, £85,890 (or about 6 per cent of the total) was spent in further fund-raising and £47,608 (or about 3 per cent of the total) went in administration. During the year 1962-3 Oxfam collected more than £2 million in cash and clothing, and in the last three years of the decade it consistently raised more than

1960 & 1970 Comparing the first year of the decade with the last to show how aid from Oxfam has increased throughout the world

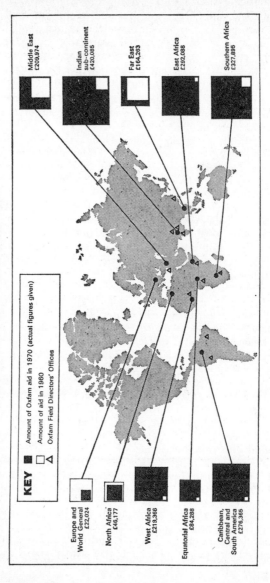

KEY
■ Amount of Oxfam aid in 1970 (actual figures given)
□ Amount of aid in 1960
△ Oxfam Field Directors' Offices

Middle East
£209,974

Indian sub-continent
£420,085

Far East
£164,263

East Africa
£292,088

Southern Africa
£327,896

Europe and World General
£22,024

North Africa
£46,177

West Africa
£219,366

Equatorial Africa
£84,288

Caribbean, Central and South America
£276,365

£3 million. This year's accounts show that about 16 per cent of the £2,926,327 collected in the UK was spent on fund-raising – including educational work – and 2½ per cent of the total supported the Oxfam establishment at home. The costs of administering overseas aid were tabulated separately, and for 1969–70 represent 6 per cent of the cash available. The Field Directorate, for instance, which costs Oxfam more than £100,000 a year, is an expensive item. It is, however, as I shall demonstrate, no luxury.

Not all of Oxfam's money comes from tins shaken in people's faces at Christmas time. To be sure, quite a lot of it comes from such sources: a young cripple swings his way on crutches from John O'Groats to Land's End to collect a small fortune for Oxfam; Inspector Barlow of 'Z Cars' talks on television for five minutes and frightens viewers sufficiently to earn 20,000 cheques and postal orders; hundreds of young Oxfammers beguile thousands of adults into sponsoring them on walks for millions of miles; there are hunger lunches and coffee mornings, fêtes and factory collections, flag days, and the ubiquitous tin. But for a good half of its money Oxfam can rely on steadier sources.

Income from regularly pledged gifts rose from around £3,000 per year at the end of the fifties to over £200,000 last year. At the height of this campaign in 1964 Oxfam raised £373,000 in a year. Legacies and covenants which were worth £50,000 a year a decade ago brought in £650,000 during the 12 months up to April 1970. Ten years ago the sale of Christmas cards netted a few thousand pounds: last Christmas they earned almost £100,000. And there has been no greater success in Oxfam's history than its gift shops. The first was opened in Broad Street, Oxford, in 1947 to sell articles brought in by its supporters. In its first year it earned £1,500. Now that it sells handicrafts from the developing world as well, the same shop makes more than £40,000 a year. And there are now nearly 300 of them. At the beginning of the decade they contributed around £30,000 to Oxfam's annual income. This year they netted £530,000.

Despite its evident achievements during the sixties, Oxfam suffers from few illusions. Its staff realises that it could make effective use of far more than £3 million a year. And it knows, too, that a private aid organisation can tackle only a few of the more urgent problems of relief and development. By any reckoning, however, £3 million is a sizable sum. I recall meeting the Governor of Casamence province, in southern Senegal, during a tour of refugee projects there. And where did Oxfam's money come from in the UK, he asked? 'Entirely from the public,' I replied. 'How much do you collect?' 'About £3 million a year.' There was a long, low whistle.

1   Following the Famine

'Old Mr Graysford and young Mr Sorley made converts during a famine, because they distributed food;
but when times improved they were naturally left
alone again, and though surprised and aggrieved
each time this happened, they never learnt wisdom.'

     E. M. Forster: *A Passage to India*

Like about 40 million other people in Bihar, Babu Govelal
Singh lives from what he grows. In a good year, he says, he
grows enough to feed the family and to sell a little on the side.
Last year was quite good, and he made 200 rupees on his surplus. At the current exchange rate 200 Indian rupees are worth
just over £10 which is not much of an annual income. I was
told after my talk with Babu Singh that he may have wanted
to impress on me how little he earned. And so last year he may
have made as much as £15 or £20. Either way Mr Singh is not
very rich.

Nor is he at all poor by Bihar standards. His four children
have not had large families themselves, and so he has to provide for only nine. More important, he is a modest landowner.
Having inherited six acres of farmland, he has acquired another four which are at present too barren to cultivate, and
he share-crops a further seven for a big local land-owner.
There are laws in Bihar to govern share-cropping which
stipulate that a tenant should not give more than a third of his
produce to a landlord. But Babu Singh needed the food and
so agreed to keeping only half for himself. At least he is spared
the iniquities of the 'contract' system by which he would have
to pay his landlord in kind whether he produced a crop or
not.

When there is work to be done on the farm, Babu Singh
hires four labourers and pays each of them £3 a month. As
cash is in short supply, they are often given the equivalent of

their wages in food. And Babu Singh provides them with breakfast – not the considerable meal to which we are accustomed, but a preparation of grain, and molasses if they are lucky. Babu Singh himself does not do much better. At the two or three important religious festivals in the year, he and his family will eat meat; otherwise their diet will be very much the same as the labourers', supplemented perhaps by a little fish and milk. Babu Singh told me that his religious convictions debar him from eating eggs.

He also owns a few animals. To be precise he has four bullocks, five cows, five calves, and, most valuable of all, a buffalo. For had it not been for that buffalo in 1966 when the monsoons stopped two months early and the crops dried out in the fields, Babu Singh would really have been up against it. He managed, it is true, by offering his land as a security, to get a small loan from the Government to tide him over the famine, but the buffalo provided him with his only source of income. He hitched a cart on to the animal and drove it round Jamui, the nearby railway town, as an amateur haulier. Others around him kept alive during the famine – as they do every dry season – by pulling big, flat leaves off the trees in the forests and selling them in Jamui as dinner plates.

There is one particularly bright spot on the horizon for Babu Singh. Last year his son, Kamla Singh, was sent by the local village council to attend a six-month agricultural course at Khadigram, just a few miles up the road from his village of Malehpur. On the two-and-a-half acre training farm there he learned that by planting crops in rows instead of broadcasting the seed, they could be more easily and more economically irrigated. Using this method, the crop could also be more efficiently cultivated and more easily secured around harvest time. Khadigram instructed him on the benefits and proper application of fertiliser, and told him of the advantages of spraying crops with pesticides. As well as telling Kamla Singh and 19 other young farmers of these things, Khadigram had them applying the techniques on its training farm, and simultaneously cultivating demonstration plots in their villages along identical lines.

By the time Kamla Singh returned to his father's farm, he had been introduced to even greater novelties. IR-8 paddy, for instance, which was developed by the International Rice

Research Institute in the Philippines, was growing at Khadigram and producing yields far in excess of any rice traditionally grown in the area. And hybrid maize, developed in Mexico through the good offices of the Rockefeller Foundation, was producing similar results. While the Singh family barely managed to scratch one crop from their land each year, the people at Khadigram predicted that with irrigation, fertilisers, and quick-maturing crops, the Singhs could be producing up to three. And what about vegetables in winter?

Fortunately Khadigram is not an academy of agricultural science. It does not exist solely to lecture on the merits of agricultural extension. The people there get their hands dirty. In 1952 Khadigram became a centre for what promised to be the most profound revolution in the Indian countryside since the days of Warren Hastings. Mahatma Gandhi, who maintained that the expulsion of the British from India was just the first step in achieving the freedom of the Indian people, had been dead four years. His teachings, however, had stimulated a generation of thoughtful Indians into continuing his work.

Gandhi was wedded to a belief in village republics, villages that would be self-governing, self-sufficient, and dependent on their neighbours only for trade and social intercourse. 'The rich man,' he wrote, 'will be left in possession of his wealth, of which he will use what he reasonably requires for his personal needs and will act as a trustee for the remainder to be used for society.' Those who have struggled to translate the Gandhian ideal into reality argue that by a redistribution of land from the rich to the poor (always mindful of Gandhi's strictures on violence) they can achieve true independence for the Indian people and challenge 'the powerful military-industrial complex which is the dream of Indian planners today'. Their movement is Sarvodaya, or Uplift of the People, and they themselves are the Sarva Seva Sangh, or those who are working to achieve unity by serving all.

At first sight this appears the sort of idea that would get little further than the minds and the mouths of its protagonists. Yet under the tutorship of its saintly exponent, Vinoba Bhave, it has done more than that. Employing that Gandhian expedient, the march, Vinoba trekked from village to village in the fifties requesting the inhabitants of each to provide land for the landless, to give up ownership of their land, and to live co-operatively. Now, like most beautiful ideas, the objective of the movement is expressed as a terrifyingly complex formula. *Gramdan*, or village gift, is said to be achieved when 75 per cent of the landowners in a village owning more than 50 per cent of the land have united to do three things: first to form a village council or Gram Sabha, second to give a twentieth of their land to the landless, and third to persuade all the villagers to give a fortieth of their income to a village fund.

The Gramdan Movement has had its successes. In the past 18 years about 100,000, or a fifth of all the villages in India, are said to have entered the scheme. Bihar, the poorest state in the Indian union and the home of Vinoba Bhave, has done best of all. By the time Gandhi's centenary was celebrated earlier this year, Bihar had become Bihardan. That is to say 75 per cent of the landowners owning more than 50 per cent of the land in villages throughout the State were fulfilling the obligations of the movement. Yet even its leaders acknowledge that they are far from achieving their social revolution. It is one thing to tot up the figures and declare a village Gramdan, another to see village democracy working out in practice.

Besides, this revolution in land tenure is supposed to benefit the villagers. Each local group of the Sarva Seva Sangh, living and working together in a community – Ashram – has the duty of ensuring that Gramdan really works. And for the villagers of Bihar, food is a more precious commodity than democracy – better to be fed than to be free. So when the rains failed in August 1966, and when 30 million people out of Bihar's population of 52 million faced hunger or starvation the following year, even Ashram workers began to doubt the priorities of their movement.

Considering the prospect confronting them at the beginning of 1967, the people of Bihar had a lucky escape that year. I asked Paras Bhai, who came to work on the Ashram at Khadigram in 1952 and is now its leader, how many people in the area died of hunger in 1967. 'I know of one,' he said. A figure for the whole State has never been computed. Perhaps a few hundred, perhaps a thousand died. By all acccounts the neighbouring State of Orissa fared far worse. It is said that they died there in their tens of thousands, largely forgotten by the publicists in the West. One famine is enough: the well-fed could hardly sustain an interest in two.

Paras Bhai supervised the provision of free food from 100 kitchens during the famine. He also organised a programme of well-digging for drinking water, and had two tankers on the go to bring water to the villagers who were too weak or too stunned to dig decent wells. The food came from organisations like Oxfam which itself worked closely with the Sarva Seva Sangh throughout the famine. In fact it was during this emergency that with CARE, an American relief agency, Oxfam mounted the largest feeding programme in its history. By May 1967, the organisation had bought 2,400 tons of dried milk, some of it in this country and some in Australia, and shipped it to Bihar at a total cost of £290,500. At Calcutta docks it was met by four volunteers who supervised its distribution in village schools in Bihar. It is reckoned that each day at the height of the famine more than 400,000 children and lactating and pregnant mothers received a mixture of American grain and Oxfam milk. Some of the less sentimental at Oxfam wondered at the time what purpose these hand-outs were serving. Sure, they prevented the hungry from starving. But would Oxfam not be returning to Bihar and doing precisely the same job in ten years' and in 20 years' time? Oxfam has remained in Bihar.

Jim Howard, who became Oxfam's first Field Director in India in 1965, recalls visiting Central Bihar in 1966. The Sarva Seva Sangh had asked for a drilling rig. 'I realised then that we had to put a punch in here.' The famine provided an opportunity. Drought or no drought, Howard thought, we're going in. That was the beginning of the Oxfam Gramdan Action Programme – OGAP for short.

OGAP is working in four development blocks in Bihar, each about the size of the Isle of Wight. They were selected because together they represent the poorest area in the poorest state of one of the poorest countries in the world. Started in 1968, OGAP was a first for Oxfam in more ways than one. It was the first time the organisation had pursued a joint programme in the field with an Indian group, or for that matter any other indigenous agency. It was the first time Oxfam had itself risked an ambitious agricultural development programme at grass roots level. And it was the first time it had supported a group of volunteers in the field. To use the jargon employed in the development business, Oxfam was going operational.

In July 1969, Ian Page was looking at the job ads in *Farmers Weekly* when this caught his eye:

29,000 acres Bihar, India. Outstanding opportunities for hard and interesting work in this famine area. Newly qualified or experienced general and mechanical agriculturalists needed urgently to replace Oxfam development team. Interest in poverty and people essential. Sound voluntary conditions for two-year assignment. Fare and board and lodging and £3 a week and £200 allowance. Apply United Nations Association.

Ian Page is a Yorkshireman with the build of a rugby prop forward. In fact it was in that position that he used to play for the first team of the East Yorks Rugby Football Club. He is also a farmer with, for his 26 years, remarkably varied experience. With a National Certificate of Agriculture and an Advanced Management Diploma behind him, he worked first on farms in the West Riding – or, as he puts it, 'out in the bloody wilds'. When he saw the advertisement in *Farmers Weekly*, he was a trainee manager on a turkey farm in East Anglia. He had thought as he read reports on the Bihar famine two years earlier that it would be a good idea to go and work there, and with his workmates had even been contributing regularly to Oxfam. He applied to the UNA, and within a month of being accepted was en route for a Hindi course at Dehra Dun in the company of three other young agriculturalists.

Page does not find it difficult to rationalise his motives for volunteering. He speaks with easy Yorkshire fluency and makes few concessions to gentility: 'I believe you should lend help where it's needed. In England you spend your time grubbing about for pennies to pay off the telly bill and that evil bloody institution the mortgage. You come to pension time and you've missed a bloody lifetime.' Certainly Ian Page has made no material gains in volunteering for Bihar. As a trainee manager on the turkey farm he was taking home about £22. 10s. a week; now he is earning £3.

During my stay in the Ashram at Khadigram, I met three British volunteers. With an Indian co-worker from the Sarva Seva Sangh, Ian Page supervises the training farm and its students. Steve Morgan, an impressively qualified motor mechanic from West London, was finishing a two-year tour during which he had given courses in pump- and vehicle-maintenance to Indian students. His trainees are now the mechanics for the other three OGAP projects. Now 24 he first thought of doing voluntary work abroad at 18, but had firm views on what sort of job he wanted: 'I didn't want to go on the VSO programme. I had no interest in teaching the rich to speak English or to mend cars.' OGAP does not worry him on that score. One of his trainees, Siyaram Gupta, now experienced enough to take on the mechanical work at Khadigram on his own, supports nine on the £6 he earns each month. And Steve Morgan has even imparted a little authentic Acton English. Siyaram Gupta says 'push off' when he means 'go'.

Arguably the most important volunteer at Khadigram is Andrew Sindle, a civil engineer with responsibility for well-digging and dam-building. Much money and much thought is going into the problems of dry-land agriculture in other parts of India. But difficult though it may be to believe during a visit to Bihar in May, the State is far from dry. It receives an average of 44 inches of rain a year, almost all of it falling between June and September. That, I was careful to say, is the average. When it falls below 38 inches a year, the situation becomes critical. For the farmsteads of Bihar are geared to an average and not a low rainfall. And so provision must be made for securing water supplies additional to the monsoon downpour. Without them Bihar will be in the queue for free food after the next drought.

Andrew Sindle arrived at Khadigram in March 1969, as the first civil engineer to be attached full-time to the Ashram. Professionally, I gather, he was appalled by the amateurishness of some of the irrigation work already carried out by OGAP. Siting dams is no layman's job. You can build a beautiful bund which during the monsoons will collect a lovely lakeful of water behind it. When the dry season sets in, you may discover that the water cannot be brought to the area which you want irrigated. Alternatively there may be seepage through the bund which renders the fields below so sodden that only a farmer growing water lilies could hope to make a living from them.

Nor is it possible to bring reliable water supplies to the whole area at once. Up to the present OGAP has concentrated its effort in 30 villages around the Ashram. By last year's monsoons Sindle and his predecessor had supervised the completion of 45 wells, six river points, four *ahars* (an ahar is a huge tank which fulfils the same purpose as a dam), and a thousand feet of channelling and piping. These structures are not brought to villages for free. To do so would be to encourage among the villagers that feeling of helplessness and reliance upon others which is the product of the food handout. If a village council decides that it wants a well, it has first to provide the labourers. OGAP will pay them for their work in food. For the concrete rings to line the well, OGAP gives a grant of 50 per cent. The village finds the rest.

Twenty-four hours after I arrived at Khadigram Andrew Sindle was taken to Patna hospital suffering from a throat infection. And having spent four days there, I am surprised there is not more illness in the Ashram. For most of the year, the climate in central Bihar borders on the intolerable, a fact that contributes as much to the impoverishment of the land as it does to the severity of working conditions for farmers and volunteers. During a summer that reaches its blazing height in May and early June, noon temperatures of 116°F and 117°F are regularly recorded. On one such day an Ashram worker casually remarked to me that if the temperature rose further, then people would begin to die. According to the newspapers in Calcutta later that week, more than 300 Biharis died of the heat while I was visiting their State.

It was on just such a day, too, that I spoke to Babu Govelal Singh. Our interpreter, one of the Ashram workers, had wound a scarf around his head to muffle himself against the hot, dust-laden wind. Standing there on crumbling earth that betrayed not a sign of moisture, it seemed almost irrelevant to ask Babu Singh whether there was any water on the farm. No, he had no well. Could he build one? No, he said, that would cost more than a thousand rupees. It appeared that a thousand rupees (£50) was the largest sum that Babu Singh could easily understand. For a well would cost between £100 and £200, depending on how high the water table was. And one encounters wells in Bihar that have been dug to depths of 70 or 80 feet without finding water.

Where, then, does Khadigram enter Babu Singh's life? One change was evident enough. In the corner of the field in which we were talking was a tiny patch of sugar cane – tiny because the water for irrigation had to be carried on to the farm. It was a hybrid variety called BO17 which Khadigram workers have been selling with enthusiasm and which Babu Singh was growing for the first time. Neatly planted in rows, it should yield enough to convince him of the value of these new-fangled techniques and these new-fangled seeds.

For more evidence we turned to Babu Singh's wheat crop which had been harvested two months before. Again, and for the first time, he had planted the seeds in rows; again he had used a hybrid. But being a conservative sort of farmer, he had broadcast the local variety in a nearby plot to detect any changes for the better – or for the worse. The result was impressive. One *kata* of the new variety (a kata is one thirty-second of an acre, sufficient indication perhaps of the size of some landholdings in Bihar) yielded 25 lbs of grain. It took a kata and a half to produce the same amount of the local variety. The result would have been even more satisfactory if Babu Singh had used fertiliser. But perhaps that will come next year. Khadigram has just put his son in charge of a small marketing centre for seed and fertiliser in the village.

The four OGAP projects – Khadigram, Jha Jha, Bodh Gaya, and Sokhodeora – have so far cost Oxfam £125,000. Some argue that this is too much to spend on an area that may be big in acres and in population, but is small in relation to Bihar – the size of England and Wales – and smaller still in relation to India's manifold agricultural problems. One sceptical economist described the programme to me as 'rather like dumping the whole of Marshall Aid on Southampton'. To this I oppose the views of Jim Howard, the Field Director who set up the project. He argues that development work at rural level must bring perceptible changes to the countryside and a permanent improvement in the earnings of its farmers. Otherwise they will become disenchanted with the very notion of development.

In theory, of course, the Indian Government has a programme of agricultural improvement in Bihar. But budgeting difficulties render it almost ineffective. There is no more than one village level worker for ten or so villages: 'You can spread butter on bread so thinly,' says Howard, 'that you can neither see nor taste the butter.' He is suspicious, too, of what might be called the pebble-in-the-pond approach to development. It is not enough to rely on one sophisticated farmer in a community to bring the message of improvement to his neighbours: 'You have to bomb the area until development is seen to work for everyone.' Self-help, of course, is an integral part of OGAP, 'but you must give a man a spade to dig a well. You can't leave the poor sod to dig it with his bare hands.'

Jim Howard has seen the OGAP brand of development succeeding. Before joining Oxfam he was the water engineer attached to an agricultural programme in Madhya Pradesh. Into one development block – development blocks are Indian Government units that represent roughly 100 square miles and a population of 100,000 – the American Friends Service Committee put £40,000 a year for ten years. Fifteen technicians like Howard were sent as well. Seven years after he left Howard returned to the area, and estimated that a fifth of the technical improvements introduced to the area were now embedded in local culture. Carrots and cabbages, for instance, were still being grown where they had never grown before. Grapes, he recalls, had not caught on.

If this can be said for OGAP in ten years' time, then Oxfam's investment will be deemed a success. True, the money will not have contributed much to improving dry-land agriculture in the State of Rajasthan. For the time being Oxfam is leaving the development of further revolutionary techniques in agriculture to others. But it will have demonstrated that new techniques, so far employed only by big Indian farmers with cash to invest, can profitably be brought to the small and to the poor. For me, the most material fact is that during a few months of famine in 1967 Oxfam spent over £300,000 providing imported food for the hungry. In the last two years they have provided cement, tools, seed, fertilisers, and technicians for the same area at a third of the price.

*

In contrast to central Bihar and the problems of Babu Singh, let us look at Mysore in southern India. Bangalore, the State capital rests comfortably at 2,000 feet above sea level. The climate is gentle and unvarying; the city's streets are ablaze with tropical trees and shrubs. When the Queen last visited India she missed out Bihar, but visited the Nandi hills, 20 miles or so from Bangalore. Both nature and the Government have smiled on Mysore. In the north of the State, the Tungabhadra dam has enabled nearly a million acres to be irrigated, and just outside Bangalore there is the fine new campus of the University of Agricultural Sciences.

Nevertheless a drought is a drought wherever it strikes, and with most of the State's 15 million farmers still dependent on monsoon rain rather than irrigation, 1967 was a bad year. So bad was it, in fact, that the State Government waived its land tax.

Oxfam has been a force in Bangalore since Jim Howard set up his office there in 1965. And his links with the area led to one of the most remarkable projects on Oxfam's books.

The issue was this. Bangalore's Agricultural University planned to start a pilot extension project to bring the green revolution to the smaller farmers of the area. Fertilisers and new types of seed like hybrid maize were to be sold to them on a loan basis through village co-operatives. Eventually, if the University's extension staff proved up to the task, the system would be duplicated throughout the State.

There were, however, two problems. First the Indian fertiliser industry was then unable to meet the demand, and a shortage of fertiliser would render the programme useless. Secondly the Indian Government would not release precious foreign exchange for the purchase of fertiliser abroad. At this juncture Oxfam stepped in. They would buy the fertiliser in England, they said, ship it to India, and collect the money in rupees at the other end. Since the farmers are repaying their loans, it has cost Oxfam nothing more than a few bank transactions.

In all 6,000 tons of fertiliser arrived in Bangalore to be distributed through the co-operatives. The sacks are stamped 'Oxfam 12-24-12' indicating the percentage content of nitrogen, phosphoric acid, and potash in the mixture. Smaller bags containing enough fertiliser for a quarter of an acre are then prepared and sold at just over £2 each. In fact, the University found itself making a small profit, and so reduced the price by 2s. a bag. Oxfam itself has derived handsome kudos from the scheme. With its name so much in evidence in the villages, visitors are regularly asked to ensure that when Oxfam makes the next lot they include a slightly higher percentage of potash. And during my own visit to the area, an

Indian vet approached the current Field Director, John Staley, to inquire whether Oxfam made pesticides as well as fertiliser.

To appreciate the extent of the revolution that capable extension workers can promote, you must talk to the farmers. Five years ago Muniyappa bought three acres of land from his employer, which made him one of the larger landowners in the village of Budihala, about 12 miles from Bangalore. At £25 an acre the land was cheap by Mysore standards and there was even a broken-down well in one of the fields. By dint of scrupulous saving, he was able after three years to afford £100 to dig out the well and to renovate the old pump set. Now he reckons to clear £150 in profit a year after feeding the family. Those three acres provide for himself, his family, his parents, his three brothers, and their families.

When I met Muniyappa he was leaning up against the door of the fertiliser storeroom at the local co-operative. His teeth were stained with betel juice, and he had wound a blue towel round his head to act both as turban and sweat-rag. Inside the storeroom were bags of harvested grain and a small pile of Oxfam fertiliser. The rest had gone. Had he used any? Yes, he had bought some the first year it was available and had used it ever since. Were the results good? Yes, he was able to harvest 220 more kilograms of grain than he had managed to get before. 'That's not enough,' Mr Hanumappa chipped in. Mr Hanumappa is the University's extension leader and was my guide for the afternoon. 'You should be using more fertiliser.' With crushing earnestness, Muniyappa assured us that if he applied more, 'the crop would catch fire.'

The staple food crop of southern India is *ragi*, a strain of millet. But Muniyappa, like other local farmers who have come under the spell of Mr Hanumappa and his fellow extension workers, enjoys a more varied diet. He is now growing potatoes, cabbages, and onions – most for market, some for himself. He finds indeed that with an assured water supply, and by fertilising the new quick-maturing varieties of grain, he can grow three crops a year where before he grew one. The most remarkable of these crops is hybrid maize. Five years ago maize was unknown around Bangalore, and its introduction was at first resisted by the farmers. Muniyappa confessed that he himself had believed the rumour that it would give him cholera. During last season he had two acres under maize. And just now he is planting mulberry for the booming Mysore silk industry. When economists talk of the necessity to revolutionise rural life by substituting a cash economy for a subsistence economy, they are speaking of Muniyappa.

*

Oxfam is doing the same job around Bangalore as it is doing in Bihar. The approach, though, is different. In Bihar, the Government's extension services are inadequate, and the Ashrams are themselves too poor to fill the gap. So a substantial investment of men and material was called for. In Mysore the University is doing the work while Oxfam has made loans to cover particular aspects of the programme. This is the role that Oxfam prefers. It is obviously the more satisfactory. The University in Bangalore will still be training extension staff after the Oxfam volunteers have left Bihar. India is their country, not Oxfam's.

Yet the gulf between Mysore and Bihar was so wide that Oxfam was prompted to act. Consider Muniyappa and Babu Singh. The first has money to invest in his land; the second has none. Muniyappa has embraced change while Babu Singh and his fellows are wary of it. If in ten years' time, the Babu Singhs of Bihar, touched by OGAP, are fertilising their crops and growing vegetables in winter without extension workers standing over them, then OGAP will have achieved its object. Even another drought in the area may prove less disastrous. And if the Muniyappas of Mysore are making more cash out of their small plots, then that supply of fertiliser will not have been wasted. It did not, after all, cost Oxfam a rupee.

2 Planning Families

'I have always said India's motto for the present
should be "Loop before you leap." '

> J. N. Chaudhuri, formerly Indian High
> Commissioner to Canada

India's greatest priorities have been expressed by her Government as follows: defence, agricultural production, and family planning. Nowhere in this book will I write about defence. Between the other two there is all too evident a link. In the last chapter we saw some of the processes that have been employed in India to improve her agriculture. Results have been good. In 1951 India produced 55 million tons of food; now she is producing well over 90 million tons a year. Yet during the same period she has become progressively more dependent on food imports. Put another way, Indians have less of their own food to eat now than they had twenty years ago. The reason is simple. From 1951 to the present day, the population has increased from 361 million to over 500 million.

Only statisticians are impressed by statistics. Let us look at the problem in a more vivid light. Australia, for instance, has a population of 12 million; India *increases* her population by that number annually. Australia occupies an area of 3 million square miles; India is a *third* of the size. There is an average of 373 people on each square mile of India; the same number of Australians *have* a hundred square miles in which to live. Or take a real farm of which I heard in Assam, north eastern India. In 1926 a farmer's son married and went to live on ten acres of the family's land. Forty years on, 28 people were living on those ten acres.

The beginnings of India's population explosion can be dated fairly accurately. From the 1921 census, it appears that there were about 49 births each year for every 1,000 members of the population. That means there was a potential increase each year of around 20 million. But in 1921 almost as many people were dying of cholera, typhoid, malaria, plague, and occasionally even old age, as were being born. In fact 48 deaths were recorded annually per thousand population. So a potential increase of 20 million was reduced to an actual increase of a few hundred thousand. Over the last 50 years two things have happened. Indian mothers are now giving birth to slightly fewer children. The birth rate per thousand population is now about 41 each year instead of 49. Secondly – and this is a fact of which the Indian medical services are justly proud – the death rate has dropped from 48 in a thousand to around 16. Whereas just twenty years ago a baby in India could look forward, on average, to a life of no more than 32 years, he can now expect to live to the ripe old age of 52.

Not only has food production failed to keep pace with the resulting increase in population. New schools are unable to absorb the new children, and unemployment is rising despite the creation of millions of new jobs. There is one solution to the problem short of relying on Malthus. The birth rate has further to be reduced.

India first acknowledged the fact at the beginning of the fifties, and has since been devoting ever-increasing sums to birth control. No visitor to India can long remain unaware of the campaign: it stares at him from hoardings and from newspaper headlines, from advertisements on carrier bags and on the backs of rickshaws; it shouts at him from the radio and from the cinema screen. The day I arrived in India, for example, I saw this item in the newspaper *Patriot*. Under the heading 'Bastar leads in Famplan Drive', it read: 'The Bastar District of Madhya Pradesh has exceeded the target for family planning programme by 5.5 per cent and has attained first and second positions in the division of the State respectively.' For further details I spoke to Dr Krishna Rao, regional family planning officer for the four southern States. We met on the feast day to celebrate Buddha's birthday, and we both considered it appropriate.

A great deal of family planning work can be done through the Government itself. Its own employees, for instance, are nudged into accepting the notion of a small family. No junior civil servant is likely to be considered for promotion if his family is large. No woman in government service will receive paid maternity leave once she has a family of three. And while the Government offers studentships and scholarships to the first three children, no such generosity will be shown towards their younger brothers and sisters.

As far as money and personnel go, Dr Krishna Rao told me that the sky was the limit. When India produced her first five-year plan, the allocation for family planning was £70,000. Now she is on her fourth, and over £150 million is available. As director for one of six regions in India, Dr Rao thus has money enough to support a variety of projects. Towards each bed added to the maternity wing of a hospital, for example, he gives a grant of £375 and then undertakes its recurrent cost to the tune of £115. For one large maternity hospital, whose own birth rate is 13,000 babies a year, he provided and equipped a new operating theatre, and installed headphones in all of the wards. These were given as much for the education of patients as for their amusement. For Dr Rao has a finger in All India Radio. There are three of his family planners attached to the local station to ensure that a little gentle propaganda is inserted into its regular programmes. Both songs and plays have been written for radio on the family planning theme.

But while money may be available, there is no shortage of problems. It is often difficult to persuade trained medical staff to take up posts in Primary Health Centres in the countryside. And sometimes family planning facilities are abused. It was not, I quickly add, Krishna Rao who told me either of the area in Madras that cooked its books to claim an inflated grant from the Government, or of the young boy who had been sterilised five times.

In some parts of India, where hostility between Moslems and Hindus occasionally flares into communal violence, the injured minority may regard family planning as a trick to limit their families, but no one else's. Dr Rao treats the issue in public as uncontroversially as he can. He refrains, for instance, from retaliating in the press to the often strident criticism of the campaign voiced by leader-writers.

As well as implementing an exclusively governmental programme, Dr Rao sees it as his duty to act as a catalyst in the community. Chambers of Commerce are asked to encourage their members to support the campaign. Dr Rao told me that the local general manager of Indian Telephone Industries had allowed half an hour each week for group discussions on family planning. Another company was providing books, clothes, and medical aid for the first three children in any worker's family.

A family of three, one notes, is the ideal pursued. It even forms the symbol of the family planning campaign in India – a red triangle suggesting not only three children, but also children equally spaced every three years. Recently, however, when the Government realised that even new families of three would not achieve their objective, two children became the norm. Dr Rao translated the latest family planning poster for me : 'We are two, and we shall have two.'

Among groups conducting their own family planning projects with government support are the mission hospitals. Indeed no other private section of the community plays a larger part in the campaign. They account for 17 per cent of the hospital beds in India, and over the years have built up a reputation for taking particular care of their women patients. Their work is stimulated and co-ordinated by the Family Planning Project of the Christian Medical Association of India. Started in 1966, the CMAI project has so far induced 230 of the 437 mission hospitals in India to participate. Others will doubtless join. But among them are a few hospitals belonging to fundamentalist Protestant sects which decline to practise contraception, and, of course, a large number of Roman Catholic missions.

One hears of Roman Catholics in India who have been sterilised, and of priests who are members of local family planning committees. But by and large the hospitals are obliged to follow the dictates of Rome. It strikes me as ironic that Roman Catholic missionaries in India and elsewhere should have done so much to introduce the benefits of medicine, and should now be precluded from accepting the consequences.

That the Protestant mission hospitals are making such an effective contribution to the family planning campaign in India is due in part to Dr Robert McClure. A Canadian missionary and nimble surgeon, Dr McClure was planning families long before the Indian Government thought of doing it. In Honan Province, north of the Yellow River, in China, he had inserted 300 loops before 1937. After his wife had given him four children, he had himself sterilised. And when he arrived to work in Ratlam, India, in 1954, he wasted little time in starting a campaign there. Believing that there is no better way to impress the populace than persuading their leaders to set an example, he sterilised an Indian High Court Judge and the Mayor of Ratlam. By 1966 he had carried out sterilisation operations on about 2,000 women, and 1,000 men, and had inserted numberless loops. That year, too, he moved to Bangalore to start the CMAI project.

Family planning came more easily to Dr McClure than it did to Oxfam. For fear of antagonising its Roman Catholic supporters, Oxfam shied away from the issue during the early part of the decade. In 1965, however, they resolved to help. Leslie Kirkley, the director, announced in March: 'We now feel that the issue of population control has become so urgent, and the resources of the specialist family planning agencies so inadequate for the demands made upon them, that Oxfam should place family planning alongside the many other ways in which it is seeking to help under-privileged people.' And to put their determination beyond doubt, they gave that month £1,725 to the Family Planning Association of Hong Kong to equip five clinics, £6,860 to the Planned Parenthood Federation of South Korea to establish and finance two training clinics, and £750 to Action Familiale Mauritius for the training of field workers.

At the same time, however, Oxfam set its face against sterilisation as a means of contraception. Again there was no doubting at Oxfam House the value and the effectiveness of such methods. But like other agencies which rely on public subscriptions, Oxfam is sometimes obliged to disdain the more radical approach to a problem. There is nothing improper in this. If Oxfam acts in a way that is thought unethical by even a minority of its supporters, the organisation will not have the money to make grants of which these same people approve.

Their objection to sterilisation became a matter for urgent reconsideration in 1967. It was during that year that Bill Acworth, Oxfam's Field Secretary for Asia, and his wife, Ausma, Field Secretary for southern India, made a tour of Oxfam projects in India. In the mission hospitals, they saw at first hand that the loop – a method approved by Oxfam – was losing favour, and that sterilisation was gaining ground. There could be little point in sustaining a programme of contraception that was fast becoming irrelevant. Sterilisation was approved by Oxfam's Field Committee for Asia and by the Overseas Aid Committee early in 1968. The Executive Committee, too, was happy to back such schemes. Oxfam's Council of Management, however, with whom the final decision rested, was at that time preoccupied during its six-monthly meetings with the Biafran emergency. Sterilisation was squeezed off the agenda, and was not finally approved until November 1969.

During the past five years Oxfam has disbursed grants for family planning totalling more than £125,000. They have supported projects in Africa, Asia, Latin America, and the Caribbean. But nowhere has their commitment been greater than in India. To date through the CMAI alone they have spent £55,000. And they have undertaken to pay 20 per cent of the programme's running costs from now until 1973. This itself is a departure for Oxfam. For generally they prefer to provide specific pieces of equipment, or to finance particular aspects of a project, rather than support its administration. Such a system makes it easier for their field staff and their office at home to ensure that the money is well spent. Missions, however, are for the most part dependent on their churches at home, and are invariably hard up. Without an adequate income for administration, the CMAI project was in danger of folding. Oxfam made an exception. Even so, Dr Isaac Joseph, the present director of the scheme, told me he would have favoured a firm commitment by Oxfam until 1975.

One hospital in the CMAI programme is the American Methodist foundation at Kolar. Some 40 miles from Bangalore on the road to Madras, Kolar is a town of 34,000 inhabitants that is noted for its goldfields. Or rather it *was* noted for its goldfields. They are now largely abandoned as the gold is too deep for economic mining.

The Ellen Thoburn Cowen Memorial Hospital and School of Nursing was built in Kolar in the thirties, and works alongside the local government hospital. Several things distinguish it from the government institution. First it is more popular among the townspeople and in the surrounding countryside, second it has better facilities – the government hospital has no blood bank, for instance – and third a doctor in government service receives a far larger salary than his Indian counterpart at the mission hospital.

The Methodist hospital has 200 beds; the morning I visited 194 of them were occupied. There are also about 60,000 out-patients on its cards. Like other mission hospitals, it has, of course, to charge for its services. A bed patient who requires special attention pays 6s. a day; if he can look after himself for part of the time he pays only 5s., a delivery costs £3 – £5 in a private ward – and so on. Those who find it impossible to pay are treated free, and this means that the hospital is constantly in need of space and cash. I quote from a recent annual bulletin : 'Now even the medical director's office is being used two days a week for leprosy and ante-natal clinics.'

Four years ago there was little family planning done at the hospital. Loops and pills and sheaths all cost money, and the people most in need of contraception rarely had enough to pay for it. Sterilisation was even costlier as it occupied beds that could otherwise be used by paying patients. It was this situation which the CMAI project, backed by Oxfam and other sponsors, set out to remedy.

The Christian Medical Association reimburses mission hospitals for part of what it costs them to provide free contraception. Each loop inserted earns a hospital 15 rupees (or just under 30s.), each vasectomy (male sterilisation) 25 rupees, and each tubectomy (female sterilisation) 50 rupees. Kolar even manages to make a tiny profit on the loops. The Government, usually suspicious of the missions, has since stepped in to make similar grants, and to issue free condoms. And for the CMAI, the matter did not rest there. With Oxfam money they bought 'Protamin', a peanut-base multi-purpose food which is rich in protein and vitamins. This was distributed to hospitals in the scheme. In Kolar, 90 per cent is given to the children of mothers who are practising family planning, and the rest used for tuberculosis and leprosy patients. It is, if you like, a bribe, and certainly a more valuable one than the transistor radios given out by the Government.

The CMAI also set up eight mobile teams of social workers and nurses to tour mission hospitals persuading them to introduce contraception and instructing them in the different techniques. There was much training to be done. Family planning became part of a nurse's curriculum in India only five years ago.

The mission hospital at Kolar is now, in the inelegant phrase used by Indian family planners, totally motivated. Each outpatient card has a space headed 'Family Planning History' under which is recorded how many children the patient has, how many of them are living, whether contraception is practised, the method adopted, and so on. Maternity ward sisters encourage their student nurses to explain contraceptive techniques to patients, women attending ante-natal clinics are lectured on the subject and mothers visiting their children in the hospital are similarly cornered. No quarter is given even to the maintenance staff in the hospital. Any woman caught having her fourth child is denied her paid maternity leave.

This may strike the squeamish westerner as both blatant and insensitive. I can go further. Of the 66 women fitted with loops at the hospital last year, only 16 asked for them through the outpatients' department. The other 50 had just had their babies in the maternity wing, and were fitted with the devices without their knowledge. The doctor responsible for the insertions was Dr Sharadamma Samuel, a soft-spoken lady gynaecologist and medical superintendent of the hospital. For her, the Indian Government's desire to reduce the annual birth rate by 11 million does not figure as large as the opportunity presented by the campaign to put a stop to the child-bearing drudgery of her patients. Both sides of the issue – the nation's and the individual's problem – perhaps deserve equally urgent attention. Dr Samuel confessed herself 'kind of bothered by ethical considerations', but had little difficulty in justifying her action:

'There are,' she says, 'two sorts of people who should take up family planning. The first are the very poor and the illiterate. They simply don't care. Then there are those who have a good income from their land. They have children simply because they need the labour. Take a woman who works all day in the fields as a coolie, and has several children at home who are actually starving. She probably has entirely irrational fears about contraception. Surely it's better to deceive her and prevent her having more children who will starve.'

Dr Samuel can deploy even more potent arguments. Many of the mothers who have their children in the mission hospital would refuse to allow them to be immunised. But they are not consulted about it. When the baby is born, it is immunised against TB and in the course of a routine post-natal inspection Dr Samuel pops a loop into the mother. The patient is asked to return to the hospital after a month for the child's second tuberculosis jab; and the loop is inspected at the same time. Last year only two of the 50 had to be withdrawn.

Nevertheless the loop will not answer India's problem. In the villages, it has been the victim of bizarre rumours. Some of the more sophisticated people will have read magazine articles claiming that the loop causes cancer; simpler folk believe that it is a worm which combats conception by eating up the foetus. It certainly can produce some disagreeable side-effects. Women tend to bleed longer and more heavily during their periods when they are wearing a loop. And for both Moslems and Hindus this is disturbing. No Moslem woman can pray during her period as she is considered unclean. A Hindu cannot mix in society for the same reason. Above all the loop is not an entirely effective method of contraception. In a minority of cases it migrates in the body, in some women it will not stay in, and in others it brings infection if unskilfully fitted.

The figures for Kolar illustrate the loop's declining popularity. In 1967, the first year in which the mission hospital participated in the CMAI project, 73 women accepted loops. The following year only 46 were inserted. By contrast, sterilisation is gaining in popularity. Among women, the figures show that there were 125 operations in 1967, 137 in 1968, and 208 in 1969. Most were done after confinements. This, says Dr Samuel, is the right psychological moment. A mother may feel then that she is through with child-bearing. Moreover for a Hindu the ten days of hospital rest after the operation cover the period when in any event her 'pollution' prevents her living with the family. For a tubectomy, hospital fees at Kolar are waived, and sometimes further inducements are offered. If a patient insists on the same treatment she would receive at the Government hospital, then she is actually paid for undertaking the operation.

With customary selfishness, the men are happier to see their women sterilised than they are to undergo a far simpler operation themselves. It takes only a few minutes under a local anaesthetic, and you can walk home the same day. Masculine prowess is, of course, quite unimpaired. Besides, one would think that a man had adequately demonstrated his virility after six or so children. In 1967 Kolar carried out four vasectomies. The first father had nine children, and the other three had 18 between them. Even that rate of four operations a year has not been maintained. In 1968 there were two, and last year three.

Above the door leading to Dr Samuel's office is a signboard advising outpatients that between 9 and 12 o'clock each Thursday morning she will conduct a family planning clinic. It went up three years ago, and will soon be taken down. The response was poor, and Kolar mission hospital decided that instead of waiting for women to come to them for advice, they would go to the villages and advise them there. The outcome was the establishment of a maternity and child welfare centre on the outskirts of town, and of a pilot family planning project in Gandhinagar.

The word 'village' does Gandhinagar a favour. Rather it is an ill-assorted jumble of mud houses forming a best-forgotten adjunct to Kolar. It has a population of perhaps a thousand, all of whom are *harijan* – outcastes, untouchables, call them what you will. Through the munificence of the local council, they were 'settled' at Gandhinagar. One regular visitor to the community is the nurse-midwife who acted as my guide. Although she has been calling there for some time now, the people still find her presence among them curious and disquieting. She is, after all, the only unmarried woman over the age of 15 that they have ever encountered. She also rides a bicycle.

My own arrival, burdened as I was with notebook and camera, excited even more comment. And among the women and children who gathered round, I selected Muniamma as a likely case for family planning. Muniamma is in her mid-thirties – she couldn't exactly say where – and her address is 'J.57 Block 63 opposite the Community Hall, Gandhinagar'. She was married – the passive conveys the point nicely – when she was 15, and has been bearing children ever since. Her first child died, but six of her subsequent children have survived. True, two of them were certified as malnourished and were fed on Multi-purpose food from Oxfam for a time. But they lived.

Between child-bearing, Muniamma works as a labourer on someone else's fields. She earns 2s. a day with a meal half-way through it at 10.30 am. This consists of balls of ragi supplemented by chillis which she must eat in half an hour. Work starts again at 11 am.

Those 2s., of course, are not the only money coming into the family. Her husband, who drives someone else's bullock cart, earns 4s. a day. Thus each week – Muniamma and her husband work seven days a week – there are £2 to support a family of eight. When her husband is ill or when she is having another child, there is less.

Muniamma is thin, her teeth are rotten, her expression is drawn, and what is left of her sari is ragged and grubby. But she retains her dignity, and would not take kindly to strangers lecturing her about India's population explosion or the shortage of housing. Just over a year ago, however, she did listen to a nurse from the mission hospital who came to call. Almost unbelievably, Muniamma is now on the pill.

The hospital has nine women in the Kolar area taking contraceptive pills. As the nurse will tell you, they are not the easiest things to administer. She has first to check that the previous month's packet is empty before issuing another. But Muniamma wanted to stop having children – 'family planning' here is a genteel euphemism – and she declined any other method. Why, I asked her, did she not have the operation? She replied that she would not have been able to lift things in the fields afterwards. She knew of women, she said, who were not as strong after they had been sterilised. This was an exaggeration, but certainly Muniamma could not have lifted anything for three months or so. And in lost wages three months would cost her about £8.10s.

It is difficult to regard Muniamma as a statistic, although that is what she is to Government planners. Let us instead take Kolar with its population of 34,000 to represent the Indian population problem as a whole. First the town's birth rate would be 41 per thousand each year. That means the increase every year would be 1,394. This figure, however, would be compensated by 554 deaths. So the real increase would be 840 a year. A little arithmetic will demonstrate that this is an increase of 2½ per cent a year. In other words Kolar's population will double in 40 years. The planners say that to keep this increase within tolerable bounds, the birth rate must be reduced from 41 per 1,000 to 23 per 1,000 by the middle of the seventies. For Kolar this would mean a real increase of 226 each year, or the doubling of its population in only 170 years. One hears of small areas in India that have actually achieved the target. But Kolar has not, and it will not be until the results of the 1971 census are published that we shall know how far the nation itself has postponed disaster.

The Ford Foundation reckon that in six or seven years of intensive family planning about 13 million couples have accepted some form of contraception. The target, however, is the 100 million Indian couples of reproductive age. And it is acknowledged that the longer the campaign lasts, the more difficult it will be to influence the ignorant, the superstitious, and the intractable. The CMAI project, of course, is small beer compared with the Government programme. They only have a fraction of the staff and the funds. Nevertheless over the four years of the project, the Protestant hospitals have helped more than 150,000 couples to limit the number of their children. Each loop fitted, it is calculated, saves the country .64 births, and one sterilisation prevents 1.6 births. So over all the CMAI scheme has saved India about 100,000 unwanted lives.

It has cost the CMAI's sponsors about £300,000. But even in terms of cash, that is nothing to the burden of which the Indian economy has been relieved. Those industrious planners have even worked out what a prevented birth saves India. The answer, covering the activities of the CMAI alone, is £90 million.

Oxfam now regards birth control as one of its greatest priorities. It is, however, an activity to which the organisation is currently devoting only about 2 per cent of its annual income. The reason is not that its other activities are considered worthier, but that there are surprisingly few opportunities for effective investment.

During the sixties, governments, United Nations agencies, and private organisations have all devoted increasingly large sums to family planning projects. So much so that the issue today appears to be less a lack of money than a hesitation among governments in the developing world about the motives of family planners in the West. This situation is unlikely to change until birth control is seen as a global problem, not as something that should be imposed willy-nilly on coloured nations. The British Government, for instance, is cheerfully coughing up for birth control programmes in the developing world, while declining to provide free contraceptive facilities in this country. Such crazy logic seems almost designed to arouse resentment and suspicion in poorer countries.

For India, of course, the population explosion is of such terrifying proportions that the issue cannot be avoided. And here Oxfam is fully and satisfactorily committed. As Jim Howard put it: 'If I had only £3.10s. [the cost of each case under the CMAI project] to spend in India I would use it to help one needy and willing mother to plan her family . . . I cannot imagine how this amount could help a poor Indian family more.' And I recall asking the present Oxfam Field Director for southern India what a loop looked like. He pointed to the ceiling of his office. There dangling from a thread and reminiscent of one of those mobiles which used to advertise Hovis in baker's shops was the device itself.

3   Forgotten People

'They say to me "I can double that begging", and
I reply "We could go together and rob a bank to
make a lot of money, but that would not be
honourable!" '

> Warden of the Association of the Physically
> Handicapped, Bangalore

All this talk of development and of Oxfam's pursuit of objectives prescribed by Governments and by the United Nations
obscures some of its most valuable work. I asked Dr Leo Liepmann, one of those who attended the birth of the Oxford
Committee for Famine Relief in 1942, what else had changed
in the sixties. 'We are now,' he replied, 'looking after some of
the really forgotten people.'

In this chapter I shall describe four projects in India that
set out to do this. The first is in Bombay where the Jesuits
run six children's homes, and the second is in Calcutta where
an Italian missionary society is providing technical training
for boys from poor homes. In Bangalore local philanthropists
have started an association for the physically handicapped,
and in Calcutta a group of determined ladies run a home for
reformed prostitutes.

On Oxfam's expenditure lists three of these projects would
earn the forlorn label 'Welfare'. It does them scant justice.
All four share a purpose larger than keeping the destitute off
the streets. They are providing what we so casually take for
granted. And not only the manifest benefits of the Welfare
State, but also the help of schoolmasters and of parents. 'Welfare' also misrepresents the relationship between Oxfam and
the projects. At a pinch, they could continue without the
organisation's help. The Jesuits in Bombay run fund-raising
campaigns in the city, the missionaries in Calcutta organise
the fairest lottery in West Bengal, and the formidable ladies

of the All Bengal Women's Union arrange fêtes and fairs and film premières. They rely on Oxfam not so much for money to keep them in business as for the capital to improve and extend their services.

1   Railway Children

Think of Waterloo Station at rush hour. Imagine, if you can, that the commuters had no suburban homes to go to: that come nightfall they would simply lie down where they were and go to sleep. Next turn the temperature up 40°, turn the clock on four and a half hours, substitute *dhotis* for city suits, and you have Howrah railway station at night. Howrah is Calcutta's main terminal, and has an unfloating population of 10,000.

I retain two vivid images of night life on Indian railway stations. The first was of a spastic of sixteen or seventeen trying to cover himself with a blanket while two yards away a group of porters jeered at his efforts. Next, as I sat in a well-upholstered compartment aboard my train, I noticed a little boy clamber down to the track opposite. With a casualness that comes of experience, he stepped up on to the railway line, turned his back to my window, dropped to his haunches and defecated. When he had finished, he wiped his bottom with a stone, pulled up his trousers, and climbed back to the platform. I know nothing about the child: he may even have enjoyed what passes for family life on Howrah station. But I subsequently met others of the same age who through the Indian railway system happened to find themselves in Bombay instead of Calcutta.

Snehasadan is a compound of two Hindu words. *Sneha* is love and *sadan* is a house. So Snehasadan means 'house of love', and was the word chosen by a group of Jesuit priests that in 1962 decided to help some of the itinerant youngsters who live around the main railway stations of Bombay. There are now six Snehasadans in Bombay, each with 25 boys, and Oxfam is providing money to build two more. With Father Jerry Pinto, a young Indian Jesuit, I visited Snehasadan number four one afternoon. On the gate there was a pretty nursery motif of farmyard animals – appropriate enough, you would think, for the under-tens.

Mahindra says he is eight, although that is only a guess. His nursery was Dadar Station, the Bombay terminus of the Western Railway. His mother is dead, and his father, Mahindra thinks, still lives somewhere near the station. But that, too, is only speculation, because a few years back his father lost his temper with the child and booted him out. They have not seen each other since.

As it happens, Mahindra did rather well for himself on Dadar Station. He wears an expression best described as mischievous innocence, and can, for a small fee, look very appealing indeed. This served his purposes admirably. With an effort he could make 10s. a day from begging. And having made it he would retire with his equally tiny accomplices to a café on the station, and blow it all on food and tea. There can be no doubt that had stronger liquor been available, he would have tried that too. But alcohol is prohibited in Bombay.

Some of Mahindra's contemporaries at Snehasadan number four lack his good looks. For them railway life had been tough. David Joseph, for instance, another former inhabitant of Dadar, is mentally retarded, and the travelling public tended in consequence to have less sympathy for him. So David fed himself on scraps, and occasionally earned a coin or two by collecting bundles of waste paper. Other boys worked as shoe-shiners, and some even ran a regular trade in fruit and vegetables. This involved picking up rotting matter from around the central markets and reselling it in the slums.

Many of the boys I met had travelled hundreds of miles before settling in Bombay. Some came in on the Western Railway, others on the Southern, and still more on the Central. One child took two years to get from Delhi to Bombay because the police kept catching him and putting him in prison. Two brothers came from Calcutta – a distance of 1,000 miles – because their mother there could not support them. They all travelled free not because travel on Indian trains costs nothing, but because their few years of life had made them good at cheating. They came to Bombay partly because it is easier to keep alive in a big city, but mostly because the train stops there.

And when they arrive they are in no mood to be coerced and regimented. So Snehasadan does not regiment them.

47

There were no locks on Snehasadan number four. But there was decent food with meat on Sundays, a roof over their heads instead of the sky, clean clothes, medicine for the sick, and schooling for everyone. Some settled in quickly. A 15-year-old called Raja, who was kind enough to bring me a drink during my tour of his home, told me he had been there a year. He was not an orphan, as his mother was still alive. But she had insisted that he find a job, and he had run away from her. At Snehasadan he continues to go to school, and hopes that soon he can start night classes in mechanics. 'A very reliable boy,' Father Pinto commented.

Others, particularly the young ones, find it harder to adjust to a sedentary life. Our friend Mahindra holds the record in number four for running away. He has been there only a few months and has done a bunk five times. 'We always know where to find them, though,' Father Pinto says. Mahindra goes back to Dadar Station, and earns his five rupees a day begging. Professionally, Mahindra is in a rut. But then he is only eight.

When the first Snehasadan was built, the Jesuits had to go to the railway stations of Bombay and find the children. Now they come on their own. Big boys often bring their little brothers. Sheikh Ayub, a 14-year-old Moslem, had heard of Snehasadan, and wanted to have a closer look. So one morning he strolled in to ask the housemaster of the home for some water. When I spoke to him he had been there for two weeks, and was soon to start at an Urdu school.

As a matter of principle, the Jesuits do not overcrowd their homes. Twenty-five boys, they say, sleeping and living in an area the size of a squash court are enough. Nor is it luxurious living. The boys sleep on the floor, do their own cooking and washing up, and keep the home tidy. Their housemasters are there to help them, not to work for them. Only occasionally are there treats. The 25 boys in number four had just spent a two-week holiday at the home of their housemaster and his wife up country in Maharashtra. Had they enjoyed it, I asked? Yes. What had they done? 'We picked cherries in the jungle, and swam in the well.'

Driving away from the Snehasadan in Father Pinto's truck, we gave about 25 boys a ride to the edge of the compound. The last to get out was a boy with one leg. He supported himself with a huge bamboo stick, but that was not enough to prevent him collapsing in a cheerful heap. As he tumbled out of the back, I asked Father Pinto what had happened to his other leg: 'Dadar Railway Station. He was crossing the lines, and was knocked down by a train.'

2   Engineers from the Slums

Not counting the chimneys, the Don Bosco School is the highest building in Liluah. On top of its four storeys sharing with the birds a fine view of industrial Calcutta, stands a statue of St John Bosco. His gaze is directed towards the spacious but dusty school playing fields, and beyond to a congested maze of artisans' workshops. Inclining his head to the right, he would see a huge scrap metal yard, and to the left a building which houses a technical school. And everywhere chimneys. The saint, dead now for 60 years, would have been delighted with the site. For among other ethereal duties, Don Bosco is patron saint of young apprentices.

He never visited Calcutta. Indeed, during his lifetime the order which he founded in Turin in the 1840s confined its work to Europe. But subsequently his missionaries, many of them with a strong technological bent, have fanned out over the world to Africa, the Americas, Asia, and Australia. They run training workshops in electromechanics, radio electronics, and a host of more humdrum pursuits. In their Calcutta province alone, stretching from West Bengal to Delhi, there are five technical centres as well as academic schools, printing presses, seminaries, and a cathedral.

The Don Bosco Higher Secondary and Technical School, Liluah, founded in 1937, now has 1,600 students. Of these, only 100 can be given a technical training as that section of the enterprise is expensive both to equip and to supervise. There must accordingly be a satisfactory procedure of selection. The yardstick employed is simply that the 30 or so students chosen each year to start their engineering training should be poor. They are the boys who will have to support themselves and their families on the wages they earn on leaving school. At no time has there been a shortage of candidates.

When I visited the machine shop in May it was high summer and holiday time. Not all the machines were idle, however. Some of the students were earning vacation pay by helping the permanent staff to complete orders left over from the term. One boy, a Chinese called Lan, was working at a grinder, and another was standing at a lathe in the corner. It had been bought six years ago with a grant of £2,000 from Oxfam.

When Oxfam gave money for that lathe in 1964, Calcutta and the industrial belt of West Bengal enjoyed a position of economic supremacy in India. And the qualifications that the Don Bosco school could give its students ensured their immediate employment. They had had three intensive years of training on machines ranging from the simple and the hand-operated – each boy spends a solid 12 months on filing – through welders in the second year – another Oxfam grant – to more sophisticated pieces of equipment like the lathe in the final year. Sure, no school leaver of 17 or 18 could command a big salary. As a welder, he could perhaps earn £7 a month. But at least it was a regular income, and he had found employment.

Now Calcutta and the rest of West Bengal is suffering a decline that would be merely spectacular if it was not also tragic. Industrial unrest – anarchy would be a better word – had resulted in the withdrawal of businesses to less troubled parts of the country. The work force is increasing as job opportunities decline. Unemployment is therefore desperately high and getting higher. Wages are currently a third less than in the rest of the country. And so on. The Don Bosco school is as helpless in this situation as the unemployed outside its gates. It can recommend only emigration to its pupils, either to other parts of India or abroad. Fortunate for them, perhaps, that at the end of their training they sit for an examination as homely as the City and Guilds of London mechanical engineering part one. It is recognised even in Melbourne, Australia, where a number of Don Bosco boys have gone.

I was told all this by Father Sheehy, a wiry Irishman from Cork who came to India in 1940 and will, he predicts, die there. Now rejoicing in the title of Economer for the Province of Calcutta, he was for some years Rector of the school at Liluah, and is still infinitely knowledgeable about its progress. He has to be. As Economer his duties demand that he find the money and the equipment to sustain all the society's foundations in the province.

There is, for a start, no lack of willingness to improvise under Father Sheehy's regime. He showed me first the 30 or so small lathes which were manufactured by senior boys for the training of their successors, and then a store of cutters and grinders which fetch £400 on the open market. And with justifiable pride he led me to a planing and milling machine which had been hauled out of the next-door scrapyard to do further service. All the metal used for training comes from the same place.

But not even improvisation and a fervent faith in the Divine will pay for a teaching staff of 75. And the Don Bosco Society receives no help either from Government or Industry. Has the society got funds stacked away in Turin, I asked Father Sheehy? 'We are beggars,' he replied. Then where does it get its money? First it has a formidable mailing list, the cards of which I saw stashed up in an office behind the cathedral. Each small gift from Europe is individually and gratefully acknowledged, and the benefactor is informed of new or planned developments so that he may give again.

Next there are the charitable agencies like Oxfam and Misereor, an organisation run by the Roman Catholic bishops of Germany and financed by special collections during Lent. This help is the best of all, says Father Sheehy. For no Oxfam grant can go astray in the mysterious way that the Indian post office contrives to lose smaller gifts. And unlike Government grants, Oxfam's help is given on only one condition: that the money be spent on the purpose for which it was intended.

During the decade Oxfam has given the technical school £2,000 for the lathe and three sets of arc welding equipment at £500 each. That, though, is as nothing to what the resourceful fathers themselves have raised in Calcutta. Three times a year they indulge in that capitalist jamboree, the lottery. Blocks of tickets are sold on the cheap to big men; big men sell them at less attractive rates to middlemen; middlemen pass them on to street-sellers, and cheeky little boys wave them in your face in shops and restaurants.

The Don Bosco lottery held last December broke all records: first prize was £15,000, and the draw was held in the cathedral grounds. It netted £30,000. There were those in the West Bengal Finance Department who thought this too much of a good thing, and unfair competition for their own lotteries.

But Father Sheehy has friends in high places. He took the issue to the official in charge, a sympathetic Marxist-Leninist, and won his case.

In theory the Don Bosco School is fee-paying. As independent schools go, it is not all that expensive. A day pupil pays 30s. a month, and full board costs £5. Few parents, however, can manage even that. Of the 200 boarders, only three are paying the full fees; some can contribute nothing at all. In between there are those whose payment is adjusted to their means. If fees are not paid on time, then a fine of 1s. is exacted from the erring parent. Miserable though that sum is, Father Sheehy is regularly the butt of vigorous pleas to reduce it. It is a concession that he always makes.

In return a tight discipline is imposed on both parents and children. 'Guardians Stop Here' reads a notice in one of the corridors. 'Otherwise,' Father Sheehy says, 'you would have parents wandering into classrooms with messages for boys and girls, or more likely instructions for the teacher.' Work in the machine shop starts at 8.00 am prompt, one hour earlier than the academic side. A list on show outside the supervisor's office records how punctual as well as how clever the trainees are. Lateness is punished. Now it is a tiny fine. In Father Sheehy's day as rector, pupils were sent home. 'That was a far greater punishment,' he says.

When Oxfam first heard of the Don Bosco school, there was a certain scepticism at headquarters. The Field Secretary wrote to Catholic Relief Services, the agency that proposed the grant: 'Is it really true that they turn out only 80 boys a year ... Would you think that the direction of the institution is dynamic enough to be worthy of our support?' A technician would probably tell him that there is a strict limit to the number of trainees who had been effectively trained on a fairly small number of machines. In any event, Father Sheehy did not strike me as particularly lethargic.

3 Enabling the Disabled

'India,' I find I have written rather naively in one of my notebooks, 'is not a Welfare State.' I shall not elaborate on this trite theme except to suggest we look at one small section of humanity, the physically handicapped. They have a hard time of it wherever they live, but take their position in our own society.

By the terms of the Disabled Persons Employment Act, introduced at the end of the last war and updated in 1958, employers of 20 or more are obliged to give work to the handicapped. They should constitute, in fact, 3 per cent of any work force. Moreover, each employment exchange in the country has its Disablement Resettlement Officer, there are industrial rehabilitation courses, and priority for jobs as lift operators and car park attendants is extended to the disabled. Nevertheless of the 840,000 registered in this country at present, 73,000 or over 11 per cent are unemployed. And this does not include the 10,000 handicapped who have to find sheltered employment. Half of them have no work. Not a rosy picture at all.

Now turn to India. It is estimated that there are 4 million *orthopaedically* handicapped there. These are the crippled, the deformed, the spastic, the paraplegic, sufferers from polio, victims of muscular dystrophy and all other conditions which interfere with the natural functions of bones, muscles, and joints. For them nothing appears to be done by law, and little enough in practice. A few industrial concerns, as we shall see, have helped existing institutions. But of the latter even, there are pitifully few. The Government has a workshop for the handicapped in Delhi, and Bombay and Bangalore both have privately-run technical centres. For those not reached by these three bodies, there is nothing but the home or the gutter. You cannot make much of a living from the State in India.

When Mr Diwan, warden of the Association of the Physically Handicapped in Bangalore, meets a crippled beggar in the street, there is likely to be a row. Beggars get priority in his workshops, and he can offer them employment starting at £2.10s. a month and rising after a year or so to £4. Breakfast and lunch are thrown in. Why then the row? The reason is simple: there is better money to be made in the gutter if you look dirty and deformed enough. 'I can double that begging,' they tell him. And Mr Diwan's invariable reply is: 'We could go together and rob a bank to make a lot of money. But that would not be honourable.' The point is taken, Mr Diwan reckons, by about two beggars in every five he meets, and they are cheerfully at work to prove it. But there is a flaw to his argument. Mr Diwan would be a rotten bank-robber. His legs are paralysed, and without his wheelchair he would be quite immobile.

He was a subaltern in the Indian army when he got polio. A military career was clearly out of the question. He lectured for a time on plant disease at an agricultural college in Poona, and subsequently found himself at an army home for the disabled in Bangalore. It was there in 1959 that he joined forces with a small group of physically handicapped and their sympathisers to start the Association.

At the beginning it was a very modest affair. First the father of a polio cripple lent his garage as a centre for training in embroidery, tailoring, and book-binding. Next Mysore Electrical Industries agreed to sub-contract a little work to occupy six handicapped trainees in the same garage. Then with the Government, War on Want (another private British aid organisation), and local benefactors, Oxfam stepped in to meet the cost of building the present centre. A machine shop was added in 1968 with money and equipment from Oxfam and HEKS, the relief agency of the Swiss Protestant Churches. Now the Swiss Government has made a huge grant of £80,000 for a more advanced workshop. When that is built, the Association will be able to employ 300 workers. At present there are 120, and it is already independent of outside funds. 'Without Oxfam and the Swiss Churches,' says Mr Diwan, 'it would have taken 30 years to do what we have done in ten.'

I suppose the assembly section at the centre looks much like any other assembly section. There are long modern work benches, with cross benches at one end to accommodate a row of supervisors. The work, too, must be duplicated hundreds of times in factories throughout the world: men and girls fitting pieces of electrical switches into other pieces, and doing unbelievable things with coloured wires for telephones. 'That's a rack for an exchange,' said Mr Diwan, as he wheeled himself to another bench. 'Oh, yes,' I said, feigning a knowledge of telephone engineering that I shall never possess. And next door in the machine room there were boiler-suited workers standing at power presses given by Oxfam. 'This machine makes washers and capnuts,' said Mr Diwan, wheeling on. 'Incredible,' I replied for the sake of variety.

If the jobs were uniform and dull, the employees were certainly neither. For some, their disability made the work slow and laborious. Others were as nimble with their fingers as any able-bodied machinist. In the assembly room, there were those who sat in wheelchairs and those who balanced on stools. Some had withered legs, some had one leg, and some had no legs at all. There were people at work whom one could not imagine working at all. In the machine shop, the disabilities were generally less pronounced. But the 20 or so young men there all took to crutches as soon as they left their machines.

Touring the centre, I spoke first to a young man of 25 called Nagraz. He had been a tailor until a railway accident severed an arm. Mr Wishwanath is 32, and had contracted polio at the age of six. He is a brahmin, but there are no caste barriers here. Mr Prabhakar is a supervisor and earns over £7 a month. He suffers from muscular dystrophy, and travelled 230 miles to find work at the Association after hospital treatment had failed. His wages are enabling him to study for an external degree in commerce at Bangalore University. Miss Hegde does the secretarial work. She got polio when she was two, and walks with the aid of a huge, unwieldy pole.

Mr Diwan manages the factory with an air of genial militarism, as befits his original calling. He never bullies, but his authority is unquestioned. Two years ago, he told me, the Association started outdoor games for its workers, and bought musical instruments for a band. So three times a week there is volleyball and badminton for the sporting, and harmonium practice for the musical. 'Voluntary?' I asked Mr Diwan. 'They have to play,' he replied without further explanation.

I do not doubt that his is the correct attitude: his rankers need guidance more than sympathy, work more than alms, an officer more than a wet nurse. As an Indian authority on the problems of the disabled has written: 'There is also a common form of humanitarianisn which surrounds these people with kindness and affection, but which tends to perpetrate the sense of depending on the family rather than enabling them to overcome their disability to live a completely independent life.'

The wages offered by the Association to these unskilled workers rise, as I said, to about £4 a month. A worker's particular disability, of course, is taken into account so that the severely handicapped can earn as much as the more able. Even so £4 is not a lot of money, and amounts to only half of what an able-bodied worker will gain from doing similar work in industry. This has caused problems. Mr Diwan has had visits from trade unionists who insist that his workers should be paid the going rate. He explains to them that his own workers are less productive than industry's and that his contractors will pay them only for what they do. 'Whatever they give,' he says, 'we have to accept.' Besides Mr Diwan is not much enamoured of charity from whatever source it comes. With an apposite use of metaphor, he says he has no wish 'to stand on any crutches but our own'.

Industry's role in the development of the Association has been equivocal. Without its co-operation it is doubtful whether there would have been any work at all. The assembly of racks for telephone exchanges, for instance, is not a therapeutic exercise: it is a money-earner both for the Association and for Indian Telephone Industries. Yet the production centre was started to provide two-year rehabilitation courses for the handicapped, not to establish a factory for their exclusive employment. Here they have failed. In the last eight years, Mr Diwan says, just one company has agreed to give work to just one handicapped trainee. There is no Disabled Persons Employment Act in India.

4 Stooping to conquer

'Sometimes when journalists come and give us a good write-up, we get lots of offers.' I was speaking to the honorary member in charge of the children's home, and she was talking about proposals of marriage. 'But generally,' she added, 'the offers come from orphan boys.' The girls we were discussing were all of high school age, and under the care of the All Bengal Women's Union in Calcutta. Some would have grown up in the home, abandoned perhaps as children by their parents; others were unmarried mothers, and some had been prostitutes.

I can well understand the interest of Calcuttan malehood in the place. The girls are a giggly and alluring lot in their uniforms of white sari and red waist band. And each morning they can be seen trooping out of the home to school. They are enjoined to ignore male overtures on the way. 'But some of them,' sighed the same honorary member, 'want to get married to the boys they meet in the streets.' If they want to badly enough, then marriages are arranged. Instead of mothers assiduously researching into the background and prospects of the suitor, as is the practice, social workers and members of the Union undertake the task. Last year five girls, Hindu and Christian, were married off, while several other liaisons remained under negotiation.

On occasions the home has been the target of a less healthy masculine invasion. Elliot Road is not the most salubrious part of Calcutta, and the house itself is adjoined on one side by tenement blocks. As one report put it: '. . . certain "vulgar and licentious" youths have made sorties against the girls by night, which, apart from anything else, has a disastrous propaganda effect.' It does credit to Oxfam's attention to detail that £500 of one of their grants to the home should have been allocated towards raising the boundary wall by four feet.

It is Oxfam's policy not to make contributions for academic education. This, to my mind, is quite correct. Being able to read or write is less important than being healthy and well-fed. So the pretty girls who go out to high school, and the 86 younger children who attend classes in a primary school on the premises are not being educated with Oxfam's money. They are supported in part by Government grants and in part by funds from other private sources. Many of the smaller children are certainly in need of such support. One little boy – boys can stay in the home until they are six when they go to a Government orphanage – retained on his neck the marks of his mother's attempt to strangle him. Another – now recovered – had come to the home with a hunch on his back, inflicted by some fiendish method to make a good beggar of him.

Oxfam's money has been used to provide specific facilities for the home. It has helped build and equip a sick block of 30 beds, and convert an old canteen into a bright new restaurant. Much is claimed for that restaurant. The ladies told me that it was one of the few in Calcutta that specialised in Bengali food, and, more remarkable, that it was the only establishment in India that employed waitresses. The girls who work there are from the home, and demure as they may seem as they bring your highly-spiced lunch, it is only the home that has provided them with an alternative to the streets.

The Suruchi (Good Taste) Restaurant is not the only enterprise which the home has started for girls who do not pursue careers outside. The sewing department makes a good profit by selling its produce from a little shop in Elliot Road, the block-printing department employs four girls making saris for a wholesaler in Delhi, and the weaving department has 22 girls at work. This also does well. I was shown the tree in the compound up to which they wish to extend the present building. Oxfam is playing a valuable double-game here. Not only have they helped the production centre with funds, but they are also buying table cloths made in the weaving section for sale in their gift shops at home. As Mrs Mira Gupta, the attractive honorary member in charge of the weavers, told me: 'It is far better to pay for these things than to give a girl five rupees and say: "There, that's from someone in England."'

My first encounter with the ladies of the All Bengal Women's Union was at Flurry's, a tea shop that does for Calcutta what the Ritz does for London. Service is liveried but unobtrusive, and cakes are transferred to one's plate with tweezers. There I met Mrs Romola Sinha and Mrs Shiela Davar, respectively the charming president and honorary general secretary of the Union. Later in the week I saw them again when I was invited to take tea with Mrs Sinha. It was served in exquisite china and with cucumber sandwiches – no crusts.

I mention this to point the contrast with the work that the Union was formed to do. Mrs Sinha herself confesses that as a young lady she knew nothing of the squalor and brutality that can surround the life of a whore. Now she makes regular calls on the red light areas of Calcutta, and visits patients in the city's VD clinics. It is not prostitution itself that they are out to stop: this, they concede, is as old as mankind. Their aim is to eliminate a traffic in innocent and unwilling young women, and to protect the children manufactured by this trade. The ladies of the ABWU can tell you of girls of 12 and under who have been kidnapped and turned into prostitutes. There are girls in their institution who have run away from home with boyfriends only to be abandoned later in the city. Calcutta offers little but prostitution to an illiterate teenager girl with no family and no home.

The ABWU started in 1932 as a political pressure group. Madras State in the south had three years earlier passed a Suppression of Immoral Traffic Act, and the ladies wanted one for Bengal. They collected 17,000 signatures, and got it. A year later they opened their home, and welcomed their first three girls. While looking after their charges there, they have not ceased to campaign for amendments to anti-vice legislation which now covers all India, and for the effective implementation of the existing laws.

In the 1940s they began employing women guides to offer advice and help to girls arriving unaccompanied at Howrah railway station. Now they employ trained social workers who visit the women's sections of Calcutta's prisons. And right through the Union's life, the ladies have kept beady eyes on other rescue homes. Some of the less efficient or positively corrupt have been closed at their behest.

In all their work, the visitor detects that perceptible fragrance of feminism, and the ladies of the ABWU are rightly proud that they are the only women's organisation in India devoted to restoring dignity to their sex. Not a man is seen in the place. They have even invented Indian waitresses to flaunt their independence.

4   Disaster in Peru

'Yungay was a most beautiful place. It was full of
fruit trees, and the people had a kind of satisfied look
on their faces.'

American Volunteer in Peru

Looking down on Huari from the hills above, it was hard
to believe that no one had been killed there. The earthquake
had dislodged heavy roofing tiles on every house in the town;
some had crashed into the streets, others had just shifted.
Walls had tumbled over choking the roads; the west front of
the cathedral had collapsed, and great cracks had appeared
in the sturdy building occupied by the local council. Schools in
the town were uninhabitable, a training centre for peasant
leaders was in ruins, a new institute for women's training was
badly damaged, and the second floor of the hospital was dan-
gerously insecure.

According to the scale which Mercalli evolved for judging the
intensity of an earthquake, the town of Huari suffered an
eight. Number eight reads in an abridged form:

Damage slight in specially designed structures; considerable in
ordinary substantial buildings with partial collapse; great in poorly
built structures. Panel walls thrown out of frame structures. Fall of
chimneys, factory stacks, columns, monuments, walls. Heavy furniture
overturned. Sand and mud ejected in small amounts. Changes in well
water. Persons driving motor cars disturbed.

Huari (pronounced 'wari': there is no 'w' in Spanish)
is a provincial capital of about 4,000 inhabitants, lying on
the eastern side of the Andes. It takes 12 or 13 hours to drive
there from Lima, the Peruvian capital. You follow the Pan
American Highway out of the city to the north, and turn off
into the mountains after 80 miles. Climbing through a mist
which for much of the year shrouds the coastal plain, you
reach the pass at Conococha at 12,000 feet, and descend into

PERU

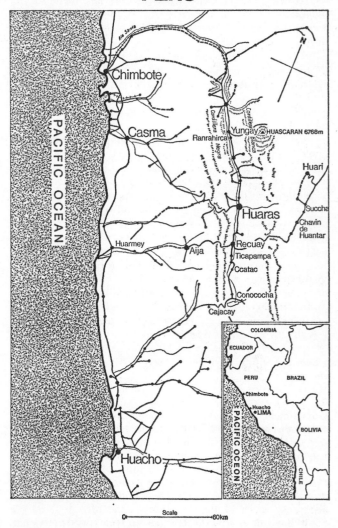

PACIFIC OCEAN

Río Santa

Chimbote

Casma

Ranrahirca

Yungay

HUASCARAN 6768m

Cordillera Negra

Cordillera Blanca

Huari

Huaras

Succha

Chavin de Huantar

Huarmey

Aija

Recuay

Ticapampa

Ccatac

Conococha

Cajacay

Huacho

Scale

0 ⊢————————⊣ 60km

COLOMBIA

ECUADOR

PERU

BRAZIL

Chimbote

Huacho

LIMA

BOLIVIA

PACIFIC OCEAN

CHILE

the Callejon de Huaylas. This valley runs north for 200 miles, and is heavily populated. On its western flank there are the mountains which you have just crossed, the Cordillera Negra, and to the east the Cordillera Blanca, a range which you must now cross to reach Huari.

Before leaving the valley, you pass through the towns of Ccatac and Ticapampa. It is then a haul of three hours to reach the Kahuish tunnel at 14,000 feet. Once through the tunnel, you twist down cramped valleys, bump over the cobbled streets of Chavin and San Marcos, and arrive five hours later in Huari.

I have selected Huari as a starting point for studying Oxfam's reaction to the Peruvian earthquake for three reasons. First it was a town where the damage was not quite spectacular enough to rate many mentions even in the local press. Secondly I was there long enough to appreciate the problems that confronted those whose responsibility it was to restore normality to the area. And thirdly it is a part of Peru where Oxfam had worked before the earthquake.

Huari's hospital has 25 beds, and serves a population of 120,000. It has one doctor, who is also the mayor, and one qualified nurse, who is also his wife. As helicopters began bringing in the injured from outlying villages, they patched up fractured crania and crushed arms and legs. The more desperately injured were taken straight to the coast. Gangrene was already affecting neglected wounds; in the nearby town of Chacas, where 42 people were killed, one man chopped off his wife's arm with a machete as it was hurting her so much. She survived.

Dr Qachay and his wife had only small supplies of medicine for such cases. And these had been rapidly exhausted. The Government had sought to fill the gap by appealing to drug companies after the earthquake. But that brought cold comfort to Huari. When the supplies arrived, they were a hopeless jumble of medical samples, some with expiry dates in 1966. There were no antibiotics, no aspirins, and no penicillin. Cerro de Pasco, a local mining company, had done better; at least the medicine they sent to Huari had been properly classified.

Although damaged, the hospital at Huari was functional.

All the injured needed was a roof, a bed, and attention. Cases of shock posed a bigger problem. Villagers whose houses had fallen around them during the earthquake were frightened even of entering another building. When I visited the hospital almost four weeks after the disaster, I met at the door a jittery little huddle of outpatients waiting to be seen by the doctor.

In the first days after the earthquake there had been more urgent priorities than cementing cracks in the hospital. For a start there was no communication at all with other parts of the country: landslides had blocked every road out of the town, and had buried telegraph wires beside them. Electricity supplies had been cut. And for its water Huari is dependent on irrigation canals from the mountains; some sections had been carried away by falls of rock, others cracked by the tremors. Nor was it as if the people of Huari are used to clearing up after earthquakes: this was the largest disaster the town had ever suffered.

By all accounts their reaction was one of disbelief and helplessness. For these are not the sophisticated inhabitants of the coastal towns, but the simpler, sometimes illiterate, Indians of the Sierra. They may live in a provincial capital, but their work is in the fields that stick like postage stamps to the hills above. Without guidance, they would have waited until someone from a larger capital over the mountains had come to help them. And there they would have waited. For it took the Government and their helpers some days even to unveil the tragedy that had struck the Callejon de Huaylas. Huari is eight hours further on.

It was as well for the townspeople, therefore, that they had Monsignor Dante Frasnelli as their bishop. On the Saturday he had left Lima for the mountains. Planning originally to spend Sunday with a fellow bishop in Huaras, he decided instead to go straight to Huari. That was as well, too, because about 10,000 people lost their lives that afternoon in Huaras, and among the seriously injured was his friend the bishop. He had run from his private chapel when the earthquake started, but was crushed by falling masonry. When I left Peru he was still in a coma.

Monsignor Frasnelli was writing letters in a room on the second floor of his prelature when the quake began in Huari.

He calculates that four strides took him down two flights of stairs and on to the patio. And there he stood for the 80 seconds of the tremor. What he heard and saw during that time was witnessed by hundreds of thousands of Peruvians over an area of 15,000 square miles: the ground bucked and heaved, walls of buildings shook in unison with it, tiles cascaded from rooftops, there was the distant rumble of rock-slides and avalanches, and when it was over a thick pall of dust rose to obscure the frightful damage.

As the mayor of Huari was preoccupied in the hospital, it fell to the bishop to form an emergency committee. This he did the morning after the earthquake, and by later the same day he had collected a work force of 150 men. Under his personal supervision, they spent a week clearing the main road into the mountains, and 24 hours restoring the electricity supply. It took a further four days to re-erect telegraph wires, and then they turned to water channels. For the rest, he drew up a list – schools first, then the town hall, and finally his cathedral. The Bishop paid his workers in food, from supplies previously given him by Catholic Relief Services to sponsor development projects in the district. But he stood no nonsense from refractory workers: he simply threatened that if the stunned and the unco-operative refused to join him, he would in turn refuse to baptise their children or marry their daughters. Reconstruction work in Huari was under way.

Of the rest of his province, he knew little. Messages had reached him from two of his priests, but from others there had been nothing. Clearly a tour of the parishes was called for, a more arduous affair in the Andes than, say, an episcopal progress from Exeter. Monsignor Frasnelli has no Daimler, but a horse which he bought 15 years ago for £20, a sum that he still considers excessive. On this he would take ten days to see the province: the town nearest to Huari, called Pomabamba, is a ride of 12 hours. The tour would inform him of the extent of the damage; he then planned to tell the people in Lima what was needed, and where.

Frasnelli is no stranger to the less spiritual side of rural development. In his three years at Huari, he has built 50 kilometres of road, planned miles of irrigation channels, and conceived ideas for rural uplift ranging from trout farms to eucalyptus nurseries. From a room in his cathedral he even runs a small co-operative that lends agricultural implements to farmers. 'The Government,' he says, 'does not get down to this level.'

Nor does the Bishop regard the earthquake as an unqualified disaster. First he believes that it will promote among his people a desire to leave the inhospitable Sierra, and move to the more fertile and less populous Montana area in the eastern foothills of the Andes. This is a migration that he has long favoured, and in which Oxfam has shown an interest in other parts of the country. Secondly he has received in emergency relief from the Government equipment that has been on order for months or for years. When I was in Huari, canteens and cookers for school-feeding programmes were cluttering the courtyard of the prelature, and he had also taken delivery of radio sets to maintain contact with his distant parishes. 'When it rains,' the Bishop observed, 'everyone gets wet.'

Some aspects of the Government's relief work had been less satisfactory. While the Bishop ensured that his own food stocks were used in work programmes, the army and the police brought supplies that were issued indiscriminately to villagers. Students at the teachers' training college, in Huari, were said to have toured the countryside giving vouchers to farmers. They, in turn, left their fields – almost entirely unaffected by the earthquake – to queue for rations in the town. No doubt they were hungry. But the peasants of the Sierra are very often hungry, and one of the dangers of a relief operation is that it will promote in people a reliance on others which is only a small step from beggarliness.

Huari is a town that, given time and judicious help, will return to normal. There are personal tragedies, of course, that cannot be repaired. I met the mayor of a village only a few miles away who had spent two days looking for his daughter, a student at school in Huaras. He had not even located her body.

And building on its earlier interest in the area, Oxfam can play a valuable part in reconstructing the communities around Huari. In fact, only a few months before the earthquake, the organisation approved grants amounting to £7,000 to provide materials for irrigation works that will benefit the farmers of 20 villages. Work had just begun on the scheme when labour and food had to be directed elsewhere. But the

65

Bishop said that the halt would be only temporary: water for a farmer's crops is as necessary as a well-tiled roof over his head. It was a sad irony that during this year, of all years, the area should not only have avoided its seasonal drought, but also have had heavy rain during the dry season. It fell just three weeks after the earthquake, turned rubble into mud, and made life in the makeshift tents of the homeless wet as well as miserable.

The Oxfam grant for irrigation channels was a standard operation. Now, with a share in the appeal launched in the United Kingdom for victims of the earthquake, they can afford to be more generous to Huari. They are, for a start, to finance the rebuilding of the hospital. A saw mill and a small brick-making factory will also be established. The purpose here is two-fold. Both operations will hasten the reconstruction work, and ensure as well that new buildings are more likely in future to withstand the effects of an earthquake. For although appearing substantial, the houses of Huari – like those in other parts of the mountains – are constructed of mud bricks called adobe. They are rarely built either with proper foundations or adequate cementing. And it requires only a moderate tremor to endanger the lives of their inhabitants.

While the town of Huari will be able to repair the damage done by the earthquake, there are other places which will have to be replanned as well as rebuilt. And there are some communities which will never revive.

I spent one afternoon at Ranrahirca and Yungay, two considerable towns in the Callejon de Huaylas. Both are overlooked by the imposing mass of Huascaran, a mountain of 22,000 feet in the Cordillera Blanca. Eight years ago Ranrahirca was engulfed by an avalanche which started in a rockslide on Huascaran. While the town was being rebuilt, its neighbours in Yungay, I am told, congratulated themselves on being protected from any such disaster by a hill that sealed the valley behind them.

On 31 May 1970, however, as the earthquake shook both towns, one of Huascaran's snowy rock-faces detached itself, and fell into two lakes below. The lakes burst, and millions of tons of rock, ice, mud, and water rushed down the mountain. Not even Yungay's hill could save it from this revolting mixture. What an American volunteer told me he had once described in his diary as 'the most beautiful town in the world' now lies under 20 feet of caked mud. The people who survived fill a few tents on the edge of the avalanche: one little community is labelled 'Campimento de Yungay', the other 'Campimento de Ranrahirca'. Reconstruction work is out of the question: two towns have been given an indecent burial, and the survivors must eventually be rehoused elsewhere.

Other towns, destroyed but not extinguished, pose greater problems. Take Huaras, the capital of the northern Sierra. When the American Benedictines, who overlook the city from their house at Los Pinos, began relaying details of the destruction to Lima by ham radio, they were not believed. Ten thousand killed out of a population of 40,000? Impossible. The head of their little community buried with a school-full of children while watching a play? Unlikely. Yet when I visited Huaras on a Sunday afternoon exactly four weeks after the earthquake, bodies were still being pulled from its ruins. Nineteen had been discovered the day before: 12 of them were the occupants of a mini-bus. And nature persisted in demonstrating its disfavour with the area. A Benedictine father showed me a seismogram which had charted subterranean activities over the previous 48 hours. Quite clearly recorded were 39 tremors.

The epicentre of the big quake was a few miles out to sea from Chimbote, the malodorous capital of the Peruvian fish-meal industry. Thus this town and its neighbours took the fullest fury of those 80 destructive seconds. In Casma, another fish town 50 miles to the south, only single-storey concrete buildings withstood the blast, scarred though they were with cracks. Adobe structures of two or three floors were razed to the ground, each one a pile of mud-blocks in the road.

It was this situation to which Charles Skinner, the Oxfam Field Director in Lima, first attended. Like the staff of Peruvian Ministries, of foreign embassies in Lima, and of other relief agencies in the country, he knew on Monday morning only that there had been an earthquake: the extent of its damage and the horror of its death toll were not yet clear. So having cabled Oxfam in Oxford and Oxfam in Toronto for money, he set off up the coast to view the destruction for himself. By Monday evening at six, Oxfam UK had sanctioned an emergency grant of £5,000 and $5,000 were on their way from Oxfam of Canada.

These funds were used in the first days of the disaster to buy supplies in Lima. Ten thousand chlorine tablets costing £100 were sent north: put in infected drinking water, they kill every known germ except typhoid. Ten field kitchens, consisting of kerosene stoves, cooking pots, and plastic cups and plates, were despatched to Casma. A month later, they were being used in the only school feeding centre yet opened in the town. One hundred and eighty children were sitting down to an al fresco meal – their school had collapsed – of soup, bread, macaroni, and oranges.

A British doctor and his team, also working in Casma after the disaster, had received a share of the £7,000 made available by Oxfam. With it they had bought food and medicine. Skinner spent £150 on picks and shovels for a Peruvian relief team in the mountains, and provided medicinal alcohol for a field hospital in Chimbote that had run dry.

As local supplies were exhausted, Oxfam began flying equipment and medicine to Peru. BOAC and APSA, the Peruvian airline, gave the organisation free space on their flights. These things were sent in answer to requests from Skinner, not on a hunch from Oxfam. There is nothing more prodigal of money or energy than shipping supplies that are neither called for nor can be adequately administered. With Skinner on the spot to do battle with Peruvian bureaucracy, there was a good chance that Oxfam's aid would reach its destination. One plane carried penicillin and vaccines against tetanus, gangrene, and measles. With these came 100,000 disposable syringes. Others brought sets of water purifying equipment, and 500,000 more chlorine tablets; 11,000 bars of concentrated protein (fruit, nut, and dates to the layman) were also bought in England, and despatched to Peru.

If Oxfam is popularly associated with one item of aid, it is blankets and old clothing. They can play a valuable role in any natural disaster. The Peruvian earthquake was no exception, rather the reverse as towns in the mountains at 10,000 feet are desperately cold at night. Before proper tents arrived, the people made homeless by the earthquake had to erect their own. Some Indians living in remote haciendas had pulled branches from eucalyptus trees to construct flimsy wigwams against the weather. They complained bitterly to me that after five weeks clothes and blankets were not reaching them. But at least the people of the villages and the towns had been helped by bundles dropped to them from the air.

In all Oxfam sent nine and a half tons of blankets and clothing to Peru in three aircraft. The British side of this operation I had by chance seen before leaving. Then the issue had been different. 'Dear supporter,' read a letter sent from a warehouse in London on permanent loan to Oxfam, 'thank you *very* much for helping us in our appeal for blankets. We have made special arrangements to see that they quickly reach those in Turkey in need of them.' For the Turkish earthquake Oxfam asked for blankets through the children's television programme 'Blue Peter'. The GPO allotted a day on which they could be sent free. Response was embarrassingly terrific: 50,000 were sought, and nearly 100,000 arrived. And more were needed later in Peru.

It is as well to make clear that after a disaster of the magnitude of the Peruvian earthquake, Oxfam can play only the smallest part. At least 30,000 people died that afternoon in Peru. The dead, of course, had only to be buried. But tens of thousands were injured, and required immediate medical attention; 80,000 houses were totally destroyed and have now to be rebuilt; 500,000 were made homeless and have to be given shelter; 500 schools were in ruins and the children have to be educated. That was the size of the problem, and the response was correspondingly huge.

The Americans sent planes from Panama, and stationed an aircraft carrier off Chimbote to ferry the wounded by helicopter from the mountains to its decks. Peruvian medical students set off within hours of the earthquake to trudge the high Sierra with packs of typhoid vaccine on their backs. Canadian aircraft joined detachments of South American air forces in dropping supplies into the Callejon de Huaylas. Shipments of corrugated iron for roofing left Australia. Each religious group in Peru from the Catholic Relief Services to the Seventh Day Adventists was allotted a valley in which it was responsible for reconstruction and food distribution. The Chileans, with tragically-earned experience of their own, sent well-equipped and fully-staffed field hospitals into the country; the Germans, lacking only the experience, did the same. Embassies in Lima, as well as channelling funds from their Governments for the relief work, raised money in the city: Brazilian diplomats auctioned paintings, and the Indians put on a charity show of national dancing. And this list does justice more to the variety of the effort than to its size.

Peruvian officials estimate that they need more than £200 million to rebuild the north; some cities like Chimbote may actually have to be moved. Of this, the United Nations has already promised £140 million as a loan. The World Bank, the Inter-American Development Bank, USAID, and other governments will provide the difference.

Yet a variant of Parkinson's Law applies in a disaster of this enormity: that a pound well spent the day after an earthquake is worth two spent the next day, three the next, and so on in arithmetical progression. This is where the private agency, unfettered by protocol and the leaden hand of bureaucracy, comes in. In the rush to fly supplies to Lima, Oxfam was beaten only by the Americans from their base at Panama, and the Cubans from Havana.

There is, however, more to helping the victims of an earthquake than waving to a consignment of medicine at Gatwick.

Charles Skinner is the only permanent representative of a British aid organisation in Lima. With Peter Oakley, who works from Recife, in Brazil, and who was sent to Peru to help him during the emergency, he is one of two Oxfam Field Directors in South America. They are far from cheap to keep there, but in the administration of Oxfam's funds they can prevent the organisation making the blunders that are an evident aspect of international aid.

In a crisis, they are invaluable. Skinner is fluent in Spanish – as Oakley is in Portuguese – with an acquaintance of Government practice in Peru that comes from serving there as a diplomat. His bookshelves are lined with Latin American histories, accounts of travel and exploration on the continent, and studies of Andean flora – not perhaps essential qualifications for relief work, but of value all the same. He also loves Peru, which is a help.

His job after the earthquake was to put this experience to use. While some contributions from abroad were gratefully acknowledged, and then forgotten by the Government, Skinner was at the airport ensuring that at least Oxfam's supplies were released and sent north. Instead of handing money to already hard-pressed Peruvian organisations, he spent it himself. He knew, too, who would make effective use of the cash, and who would not. Even more important, he was known by those in Lima who, once given the means, could themselves bring relief to the injured and to the homeless in the Sierra.

Oxfam does not provide its Field Directors with a full-blown secretariat to carry out such work. It pays for just one secretary who, in Skinner's case, is his wife Jane. Her role in the emergency was one of buying supplies, of manning the office during her husband's absences in the north, and of contact by telex and cable with Oxford. When Skinner returned to England after five weeks to discuss ways in which Oxfam could help in reconstruction work, his wife was alone. She allowed herself one departure from usual office practice. Instead of ending messages with the abrasive signature 'Skinner', she signed herself, 'Love, Jane'.

It was not only Oxfam's own contribution to relief work which its Field Director administered in Lima. Much private help from members of the British community was channelled through the office. War on Want, with no representative in Peru, relied on Skinner to see that a young public health inspector whom they sent from England found respectable employment in the mountains. He could speak Spanish and had some relevant qualifications. There were others who more sorely exercised Skinner's patience. It would be invidious to name them as the point to be made is a general one: that sympathy, even if transported half-way round the world, is not enough. Better to give the price of your air ticket to Oxfam than to go yourself. Put another way, help given to a country after a disaster like the Peruvian earthquake services an equation which must be seen to balance. On one side, there is the money invested to mount a particular operation; on the other the benefit brought to the suffering. If the equation does not balance, then money has been ill-spent.

The equation was in Oxfam's mind when the organisation considered sending its own team to Peru. It had to be sufficiently self-contained not to be an embarrassment to workers already in the field, it had to be composed of people with skills relevant to the situation and there had to be someone in Peru who could ensure that it was well used. This last condition was fulfilled in the Oxfam Field Director, who, after hesitation, requested its help. The team joined a group of American Peace Corps volunteers under the direction of Mac Ashby, a Methodist missionary who had left Lima to co-ordinate relief activities in the Huarmey Valley, 250 miles north of Lima.

On the face of it, too, the team was well chosen. It was led by Tim Lusty, a doctor and a farmer who had worked earlier in the year with an Oxfam team in Nigeria. There was another doctor, three nurses, three members of a Civil Defence group from Bristol, and two members of Oxfam's regional staff, one of whom had worked before as a volunteer in South America. The Bristolians had had previous experience of earthquakes: they had been sent by Oxfam to help after similar disasters in Turkey in 1966, and in Sicily two years later.

They left England on 14 June, a fortnight after the earthquake. In retrospect it was too late as by then most of the urgent medical work had been done. This was not sloth on the part of the team. Indeed they were given only three days' warning of their departure. But Oxfam waited on a request for assistance from Skinner, and until the second week of the emergency he was not confident that he could find a support group for them. For even doctors have to be led to the injured, and doctors who do not speak Spanish need interpreters.

The team moved first to Cajacay, a town of 5,000 at the head of the Fortaleza valley. The earthquake had caused 26 deaths there, although the carnage was not as terrifying as it might have been. A footall match had been arranged that afternoon between the married and unmarried men, and the spectacle had accounted for most of the townsmen being in the open during the tremors. In the days that followed, the town received sparing, but effective, help. A Peruvian team had brought medical attention, and a group of American Mennonites had settled in with the intention of rebuilding the town in six months. By contrast, the Oxfam team was there six days, and the medical emergency was past. But the Civil Defence workers, helped by the Peace Corps Volunteers who spoke Spanish, brought some relief. They converted a covered yard into a makeshift school, assisted the Mennonites in building a medical post, uncovered a bread oven, and taught the townsfolk to play cricket.

I met the team in Aija, a dazzlingly pretty village wedged at the bottom of a valley and obscured from on top by a sea of eucalyptus trees. Everyone agreed that it was a fine spot for a camp. Aija had suffered five deaths, and all the houses were damaged; in fact an official survey of the area revealed that only between 2 and 4 per cent of buildings were habitable. Tents made of blankets and polythene lined the streets, one of them crammed with statues and reliquaries from the church. In the hamlets and haciendas round about, the situation was worse; destruction had been total, and there were neither blankets nor strips of polythene for tents.

As in Cajacay, however, there was little medical work for the team. That was being taken care of by Project Hope, a breezy group of American doctors and nurses which had flown in from Colombia. Project Hope was treating about 70 patients a day, not at this late stage for broken bones, but for rheumatism and bronchitis, contracted from lying on the cold ground. They were also conducting immunisation campaigns against measles – a humdrum enough disease in England, but a killer in the Peruvian Andes where, ironically, it had been introduced by relief workers.

Again, the Civil Defence workers brought some help to the more remote communities. In one village, David Frame, a member of the team, built a demonstration house. Constructed with only a little cement – rarely employed in traditional architecture – with smaller adobe bricks than is customary and with firmer foundations, it would be more likely to withstand the impact of another earthquake. A veteran of two earthquakes, Frame brushes aside the difficulty of communicating in strange languages. 'They speak Spanish, Italian or Turkish,' he says, 'and I speak Birmingham English. There's no problem.'

Nevertheless, in the month the team was in Peru, the lack of building materials precluded any ambitious programme of reconstruction. For in the quantities required, they would have to be supplied by the Government. And up to the time of my departure, the Peruvian authorities were doing little more than conducting laborious surveys of the damage.

Most members of the team were frustrated. They had come

expecting energetic employment, and left with few achievements to call their own. David Frame calculated that he had done three days' work in the first fortnight. Dr Lusty was disappointed, too. True, he had saved one life, by cutting an ugly abscess from a child's groin in Aija, but that had nothing to do with the earthquake. 'On balance,' he said, 'we should not have come. But perhaps it is better to be on the spot and not needed than to be needed and not to be on the spot.' Charles Skinner, whose dry humour illuminated a thoroughly practical response to the problem, remarked as we left Aija: 'Here you have an illustration of the disadvantages of going operational.'

Oxfam is happy to take risks, and delighted when a risk pays off. But as a trustee of public money, it also hates failure. There was a risk that the team sent to Peru would not achieve as much as was hoped, and, in the event, the risk perhaps should not have been taken. By the same token, it can learn from the experience. Next time, Oxfam may approach a great natural disaster differently.

Already alternatives are being discussed. There is first the suggestion that Oxfam should recruit in this country specially well-qualified individuals who are prepared at a moment's notice to help in a disaster. Thus for the next earthquake in the Andes, there would be a group of, say, Spanish speaking doctors or of agriculturalists with a particular knowledge of these mountains. Working at altitude can be a debilitating business for the inexperienced, as members of the team found out. For the next typhoon in Pakistan, there would be an Urdu speaking team, and so on. Another suggestion is that the Field Directors, overburdened though they already are, should raise local groups which would go to work under the Oxfam banner. Either way, the organisation feels that its supporters demand of it an effective response to disaster. And money is not all that this country has to give.

5   Living Hills

'They say that if you were to iron Peru out, it would
be the largest country in the world.'

   Charles Skinner

In Oxfam's annual report for 1961, there is a graph showing
where its money had gone in the preceding 12 months. Europe
took £40,000, the Near East £130,000, Africa £470,000, India,
Pakistan and Nepal £100,000, and Hong Kong, Korea, and
the rest of the Far East £140,000. Then there is an item
marked 'Other'. About £10,000 was sent to 'Other' which
comprised Central America, South America, and the Caribbean. In a similar display prepared for this year's annual report, Central and South America alone received almost
£280,000.

   During the sixties Oxfam has become as committed in
Latin America as it is in other parts of the world. Two Field
Directors, as we have already seen, now divide the area between them. Peter Oakley works in Brazil, a country so vast
that he concentrates on the impoverished north-eastern region
around Recife, and Charles Skinner's empire covers Colombia, Ecuador, Peru, and Bolivia. They assess and report on
projects there that are as varied as Oxfam's work elsewhere. In
this chapter I shall describe two, both of them in Peru. One is
an ambitious programme of rural education in the south, the
other a contribution to welfare work in the slums of Lima.

1   Revolution by Radio

As far as I am aware, there is no census of radio stations in
Perù. Such a survey would certainly be difficult to conduct. In
Lima alone there are at least 30, complementing five television channels. In the countryside each town worth the
name – and some that are not – boasts a station. Most are

privately run, earning a living from advertising, and others are controlled by the Government, supporting themselves in the same way. There are also religious stations which insert lustreless messages from the saved between the advertisements and the pop. The Roman Catholic Archbishop of Lima is even said to have his own. At present it shuns propaganda, but should his co-religionists ever be persecuted, he will have an admirable platform from which to combat the forces of evil.

Stations that seek to do more with their air space than pump out pop are frowned upon. By Peruvian law, 'cultural' radio cannot accept advertisements. Moreover, they are obliged to use the short wave band, meaning that their listeners have to buy special radios not ordinarily on the market. This will soon change. The new Government in Peru is to give them wavelengths on the medium band, and allow them to accept advertisements. No station will benefit more from this reform than Radio Erpa which is now broadcasting from Cañete, 120 miles south of Lima, on the short wave band.

Erpa stands for Escuelas Radiofonicas Populares Americanas, or Radio Schools for the People. Started five years ago by Roman Catholic priests in the province, it is now run by a lay organisation called Prosip, or, to give it its full and grandiose title, Promotora de Obras Sociales y de Instruccion Popular (Society for the Promotion of Social Welfare and Popular Instruction).

From Cañete on the coast, Radio Erpa's powerful transmitter reaches three provinces, and altitudes ranging from sea level to 12,000 feet. Most of its audience lives in areas where there are no schools, no doctors, and no hospitals. Some of the mountain communities have only mule tracks to connect them with their neighbours. And the roads are bad enough : one province, an area of a few thousand square miles, has two which, as a member of Prosip blandly put it, 'have some discontinuities during rain time'.

There are 174 radio schools operating in the area, with an average attendance of 20. In one sizable town near the coast, there is a radio school with 72 students; in the district of Ticllacocha, at a height of 11,500 feet in the Andes, four shacks of shepherds also have one. But that has only six students. Facilities are the same for both – a transistor radio, a blackboard, benches and tables, kerosene lamps, books, and a cabinet in which the equipment can be stored after class. They are not, it is clear, the most lavishly equipped of schools. Indeed, without the books and the radio set, Prosip calculates that it costs on average only £21. 10s. to establish a school. What else do you need except a teacher and the will to learn?

Radio Erpa is self-help at its best. The villagers have to provide a building for the school, and make all the equipment for it. Only the uncarpentered wood is provided free. When lessons start, the accent is on how villagers can themselves improve the standard of living in their community, not on how Prosip's technicians can improve it for them. The teaching is severely practical. Programmes are broadcast on compost, not Spanish literature, on farming co-operatives, not Latin American history, on insecticides, not arithmetic, and on dressmaking, not elocution. I have in front of me one of Erpa's publications. Not much of a grounding in Spanish is required to translate at least the last three words of its title: 'Evite Enfermedades Usando Una Latrina.' With the aid of a bold diagram on the front cover, it traces the progress of a fly from cattle dung to an ill-constructed lavatory, through 'manos contaminadas' to the dinner table, and from there to an 'enfermo' in bed, and so to the grave. Inside there are more wholesome pictures showing how latrines should be built. On the back is the legend 'Donativo de Oxfam.'

Prosip realises, of course, that for many of the smaller and less sophisticated villagers in the mountains, it must do more than provide schooling and literature. So its technicians, some Spanish and some Peruvian, regularly tour the area by horse and by landrover from their station at Cañete. They tell new villages about Erpa, acquaint themselves with specific problems and ensure on their return that these issues are tackled in the programmes. There is little point, too, in telling peasants about the advantages of spraying crops unless sprayers are available. And many are too poor to buy them. With Oxfam's help Prosip is accordingly providing implements for the trusted and for the attentive. Not only handsprayers are available. There are also small looms for weaving, scissors for cloth-cutting, and beehives for honey, a valuable addition both to a villager's income and to his diet.

To promote among isolated villages the feeling that they

are part of a wider community, Prosip runs a small magazine and arranges competitions by radio. The best village after a two-month course of programmes receives a set of agricultural tools, provided by Oxfam. And what Prosip itself has learnt over the past five years is now being put to use in training courses for promising farmers, supported by Oxfam. There are also plans to start processing plants and marketing centres for village produce.

No one who has thumbed through the mail arriving at Radio Erpa would doubt the value of its work. I spent a quarter of an hour doing so, and found, quite at random, this collection of comments and queries. 'How exactly do you make sweets out of peanuts?' asked one listener. As often as not a whole class had signed an elaborate document, drawn up after the fashion of Imperial Spain, and sent it to the station. 'Could you please,' wrote the people of one town, 'do your programme a little more slowly and clearly?' Labourers on a hacienda near Cañete made the same point: 'Please go slower in the programmes about first aid so that we can take the important points down.'

'We have decided to start raising chickens at 10,000 feet,' began another letter. Hacienda Casa Blanca wrote: 'How and when do you vaccinate rabbits?' The last two points are more remarkable than they may appear. For it is certain that before Radio Erpa started, raising chickens was a matter of giving a few scrawny birds the run of a village, and raising rabbits unheard of.

There were more letters. From a mining town high in the mountains, one radio pupil wrote: 'I am in charge of growing pumpkins for our new co-operative. When are the fruits ready to pick?' Some correspondents had produced lists of queries, others had written just to thank the radio station: '... for this you have our eternal gratitude.' My favourite question ran: 'Is it a superstition that if you plant lucuma on its own, you will die? Should you plant it with a cat's paw?' Lucuma is a fruit, and the answer given by Radio Erpa was straightforward: 'It is only a superstition. You should not believe it.' Generally questions are answered over the air by the Prosip staff, and confirmed by letter. If they need expert help, they have friends in the experimental Agricultural Station at

Cañete or in the Veterinary School at Chincha, a few miles down the coast, who can provide it.

For further proof of Radio Erpa's effectiveness, I drove one afternoon into the mountains to see a school in session. My companions included the secretary of Prosip, a young Peruvian industrial engineer who works voluntarily for the organisation, and two full-time members of the staff, one from Spain and the other from Andorra.

Even as we passed through the vast and now nationalised sugar estates on the outskirts of Cañete, the tiresome coastal fog left us. There was revealed instead a valley of consummate beauty. Towering to the left and to the right were the foothills of the Andes, lifeless except for the occasional wiry shrub. But on the floor of the valley, the Cañete River had thrown up fields of yellow corn and vegetable gardens and dense little fruit orchards wherever it splashed. Its waters were carefully conserved: by the side of the road ran channels fed by the river to irrigate crops further afield.

Following the Cañete we first reached Lunahuana, a town as lovely as its name is euphonious. Its patios and covered walks stand on a promontory of rock overlooking the river, and command spectacular views of the valley. It is also the centre for courses run by Prosip for village leaders. From here we drove on and up for two hours to reach the village of Chavin, our destination. By this time it was dark, and the evening broadcast was about to begin.

Chavin is just off the main road. To be precise, it is the other side of the river, and there is no bridge at this juncture. The villagers have instead erected a taut steel rope which spans the Cañete at a height of six or seven feet. On this is slung a wire basket, large enough for two adults to propel themselves across. It is, however, in the nature of a wire basket not to be on both sides of a river at the same time, and rarely to be on your side when you most need it. Wary villagers, moreover, tend to keep wire baskets on their side of the river after dusk. We were helpless.

Espinozo was the man whose attention we had to attract. It was he who had been instructed to welcome us. We stood on the bank and screamed 'Espinozo!' in unison. Silence. Espinozo was learning about insecticides.

Some minutes after the lesson had ended in Chavin, a villager and his family walked from the main road to our station on the bank. With a casual glance in our direction, he undid his belt, flipped it over the wire, did it up again, and raced across. When he returned, he was towing the basket. Into it first went his family and then their belongings. Thereafter, in an orderly if lengthy progress, we too crossed the wire, and walked up into Chavin.

The village has a population of 170. Of these, 20 men and women are enrolled with Radio Erpa. The classes are held in the primary school, which the villagers themselves built 15 years ago, and are conducted by Señora Elena Luján, the schoolmistress, whose salary is found by the Government. It has found little else for Chavin. 'In our dreams we see a bridge,' said Señora Luján after explaining that all village produce – cotton, limes, lemons, oranges, and apples – had to cross the wire to market. 'Then,' she continued, 'we want some defence against the floods which wash us out every rainy season.' As an afterthought she added: 'And our church has no roof.' The requests appeared reasonable. Each landowner in the village is, after all, dutifully paying tax to the Government.

Radio classes have been held in Chavin for the past four years. Had they been useful? Señora Luján gave me a list of benefits as an answer, and villagers standing around her murmured in agreement. They were preparing compost which had never been made before, she said, and some of the villagers were using insecticides on their crops. Prosip had given the village a handspray. Señora Luján had herself followed the gardening broadcasts closely, and had started a small vegetable garden. Some of the women thought the programmes on family hygiene and first aid the most useful – particularly as the nearest clinic was at Cañete, three and a half hours by truck down the valley – and one farmer told me that the arithmetic lessons had helped him to keep better accounts.

Prosip had provided the village with a few beehives which I was shown by the light of a kerosene lamp. Yes, they said, they were getting some good honey from them, but they were also getting stung. The Prosip man told them that, with more experience, they could avoid that. I did not have to ask whether Oxfam had helped. Stamped on the top of the blackboard in white lettering was 'OXFAM – ERPA'.

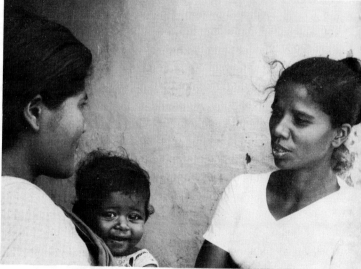

Top: Well-digging in progress on an Oxfam development project in central Bihar.

Bottom: A nurse-midwife talks to a mother about family planning near Kolar, southern India.

Left: An Indian farmer shows off his crop of hybrid maize in a village near Bangalore.

Top: Brother Molines, a Spanish Jesuit, jokes with the orphan boys of one of the Snehasadans (Houses of Love) in Bombay.

Bottom: Knocking-off time at the workshops run by the Association of the Physically Handicapped in Bangalore.

Top: Searching for lost relatives in the ruins of Huaras after the Peruvian earthquake of May 31, 1970.
Bottom: Monsignor Frasnelli, the Bishop of Huari, talks to townsmen outside the ruined West Front of his Cathedral.

Top: Villagers attending evening classes at a radio school in the mountains of southern Peru.

Bottom: Eric Rempel, a Canadian volunteer in Botswana, instructs his agricultural students in the dehorning of cattle.

Above: Brother Schrenk of the Society of White Fathers tells one of his young Ghanaian farmers about an addition to their agricultural armoury.

Top and bottom right: The dead and the barely living: cattle in Niger, West Africa, June 1970.

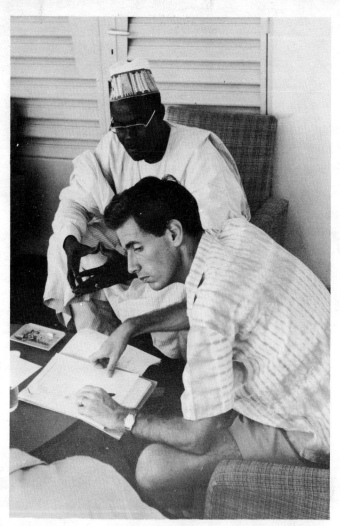

Above: Bill Jackson, Oxfam's field director for West Africa, discusses a well-digging project with the prefect of Maradi, central Niger.

We left Chavín as the moon was rising. Its light threw the tops of the mountains into vivid silhouette, and cast a pale glow on their barren slopes. I had two regrets. First I had not seen the village in daylight, and secondly I had not watched a class at work. That was put right the following afternoon. On our way to Lima, we called in at Cerro Azul, a small fishing town on the cold, foggy coast. Asking for Casa de Arona (Arona's house), we were led to a one-room building set a little apart from its neighbours in a dusty compound. Inside on a shelf was a Philips transistor, and around it trestle tables and benches. There was nothing else except a bare light bulb, hanging from the ceiling.

This was the 3.15 broadcast, and the subject was dressmaking. Fifteen or so women sat taking notes or stood to cut out patterns. Their children were only moderately restless by their side. You would think that a bunch of foreigners entering the room would have disturbed them. But there were only the most perfunctory looks in our direction. We spoke to no one in the class. They had more important things to do.

2 By the Poor for the Poor

In India they call them *bustees*, in Tunisia they are *gourbivilles*, in Turkey *gecekondu*, in Mexico *colonias proletarias*, in Venezuela *ranchos*, and in Peru *barriadas*. In Glasgow, in Londonderry, and in Liverpool they are slums. No one slum, of course, is quite like another. From city to city, they vary both in size and in standard. There is indeed only one factor that unites them. In each case they are populated by the poorest members of society.

Before turning to some hopeful stirrings in the barriadas of Lima, let me record two occasions in India. For there the population explosion has been felt even more severely in the cities than on the land. I spent one afternoon with Father Sheehy, of the Don Bosco Society, in the backstreets of Calcutta; and in Bombay some of the less pleasant sights were pointed out to me by Father Pinto, the Jesuit. It is not mere fortuity that I should have been accompanied both times by priests. As we shall see in Lima, it is very often they who bring the most valuable help to the people who most need it.

Not far from the Roman Catholic Cathedral, in Calcutta, is

an area known as Chinatown. Populated, as its name suggests, by Chinese immigrants, its narrow, filthy streets used to be obscured from view from the main road by blocks of flats. 'Flats' is a misnomer: in reality single rooms, small and airless and reached by rickety staircases. In each there was a family, or, more likely, a number of families. So hot and stuffy did they become during summer that many occupants chose to join the countless thousands of Calcuttans who each night sleep on the city's pavements. Nevertheless these blocks provided a decent shelter during the monsoons, and somewhere to keep pots and pans throughout the year.

A few years ago these houses were pulled down to build offices. Their owners were compensated. Not so their tenants. Nor was any alternative housing provided for them. Some moved to other parts of the city; the ones I saw had stayed there. They now inhabit little shacks, made of sticks and roofed with cardboard and paper which are set down on vacant land near the new offices.

Now hovels are hovels the world over, and it is often difficult for the stranger to summon up the sympathy that their occupants deserve. Father Sheehy prompted me: 'You see that birdcage there?' He was pointing to a long wooden box, the size of a coffin, and raised a few feet above the ground. One end had a tiny door made of wire mesh. 'Someone will sleep there tonight.' 'At least,' I replied, 'he hasn't got a landlord now.' 'Don't you believe it,' said Father Sheehy. 'Someone owns the land where that thing has been put. And he comes round every month collecting 5 rupees to prove it.' Five rupees make between 4s. and 5s., a substantial sum if you earn no more than that in a week.

Next to Bombay. They were laying new water mains when I was there in May. Lengths of piping, large enough for a man to stand up in, were strewn along the road to the airport. And men *were* standing up in them. At one road junction I caught sight of a piece of coconut matting hanging over the end of a pipe. The other end was similarly sealed off. Father Pinto confirmed that there was a family living there.

Airport roads generally tell one quite a bit about a city. In Bombay the authorities have even tried to rehouse people from the slums which disfigure its approaches. Rooms in the new blocks cost no more than a few shillings a month. Yet the

Government has failed to entice bustee-dwellers into them. There have been those who have moved for a few months, and then drifted back again to the slums. It is not that they have any love for these rotting and infested areas; it is simply that for their livelihood they depend on them. Every third or fourth house has something to sell to its neighbours: in some it is food, in others it is illicit liquor, and in a few it is prostitution.

The same is true of the barriadas of Lima. A rehousing programme there would solve no problems. It would merely recreate the same problems in a more pronounced form elsewhere. For what has happened in Lima is that virgin land on the outskirts of the city has been colonised by the inhabitants of the impoverished and overcrowded centre. The results may be unappealing to an aesthetic eye; but the communities are there to stay, and as they become entrenched, the job of the Government and of the charitable agencies is to help them, not to impede their progress by uprooting them.

Twenty-five years ago the barren hills which encircle Lima on the north, on the south, and on the east – to the west is the Pacific – were empty. The city's population was confined within them. It was, however, growing at a fantastic rate. There was first a steady decline in the death rate, compensated by no such decrease in the number of births. This process was aggravated by the migration of landless labourers and small farmers from the countryside to the town. For in the mountains and in the big estates, numbers were also increasing. And there insufficient land or lack of employment meant starvation. In the town there was at least a chance of work. So they came, as they continue to come, thousands of Dick Whittingtons each year.

Most avoid starvation. But work is not plentiful, and the city's streets, though providing some sort of living, are certainly not paved with gold. Rooms and houses are also expensive. It was therefore an alliance of desperation and sound enterprise that stimulated the settlement of those cheerless hills, and still stimulates it today. The first small colonies were short-lived as the police drove settlers back to the city after rounds of burnings and beatings. Then the invaders realised that there was a certain safety in numbers, and new settlements were secretly and elaborately organised. They

selected land that was owned by some public agency, preferably the Government itself; private landowners, they argued,
would defend their holdings to the last, and the evidence suggests that they were right.

Having chosen a site for their colony, the organisers would
visit it at night to mark out plots for individual homes and to
locate streets, shops, and even schools, churches, and clinics.
As often as not they would appeal for support to a sympathetic churchman or politician, and tip off friendly newspapers so that the reaction of the police could be well
reported. On a given day the invaders, sometimes in their hundreds and occasionally in their thousands, would rush the
hill in taxis, in trucks, in buses, and on bicycles. They would
hastily erect shelters on their lots, and then stand to repel
boarders. The Government was never sympathetic, but to
avoid trouble usually refrained from attacking the communities once they were established. Since the late forties there
have been more than a hundred invasions of this type. No
accurate estimate has been put on the number of people now
living in the barriadas. But it certainly runs to well over
500,000 and one missionary told me that, counting all the
shanty towns both inside Lima and on its outskirts, they accounted for a half of the city's $2\frac{1}{2}$ million people.

Each barriada has its own character. Of the three I visited,
El Agustino was the oldest and the most densely populated.
It is built on a hill which stands on its own close to the city.
Thirty years ago there was no one living on it, not even at its
base. In 1946, it attracted its first residents from the central
slums when the shanty town of San Pedro was constructed.
San Pedro now has 634 families who have just celebrated
their twenty-fourth anniversary. But though proud of their
length of tenure, they are by no means the only people who
have stepped up, both literally and metaphorically, on to the
slopes of El Agustino. Brother Tony Carbone, of the American Sons of Mary who work there, says that the city side now
supports a population of 120,000, and the far side 80,000.
And its population is growing by the week.

There is no natural terracing on El Agustino. Its inhabitants have had to hack roads and platforms for their houses
out of rock and rubble. The structures at the bottom are now
made out of brick and mortar, the product of savings over the

years. Some boast a proper water supply, electricity, and even television. Further up, the picture changes. This is where the more recent arrivals have squatted. There are no roads here, just steps cut in the rock; there is no water except that brought in buckets from tankers which tour the barriadas; there are no drains except for the natural slope of the hill; there is certainly no electricity and the houses are built out of *esteras*, the local word for woven matting.

As income earners bring money on to this part of the hill, the situation will doubtless improve: esteras will give way to bricks. But even as this happens, there will appear yet a higher and a poorer layer to El Agustino. Newcomers are already being forced out along sandy spurs of the hill, areas used before as rubbish tips, and have money when they arrive for just a windbreak.

Almost all that the residents of El Agustino have achieved has been by their own toil. Brother Carbone gave me two examples. They wanted a water tank, he told me, but the Government either would not or could not provide one. So they built it themselves. They wanted a police station, but the Government said they could make do without. So they built one and equipped it and the Government was obliged to send policemen to man it. Economically, in fact, they are independent of the Government, as they have to be to survive. They receive no security benefits and no help with their houses. True, there are a couple of Government agencies which share a responsibility for the barriadas. But they have money problems of their own, and can offer only the mildest of palliatives.

Sociologists suggest that this very neglect by Government has contributed towards the dynamism shown by some barriada communities. To move them, even to step in and direct or manage them, would be to retard what has been a natural and a vigorous development. For the barriadas are democratic places, perhaps too democratic for some of the Governments that have ruled Peru in the last 20 years. They hold elections for local councils, choose their own mayors, and enjoy a form of local leadership that reaches down to the poorest mat hut. Some of their menfolk earn decent money in the city, and others look for work that they do not always find. The barriadas themselves are hives of private enterprise. Setting up a little shop is one way to make money, but less conventional methods are also used. A resident may invest in a water tank so that he can supply his neighbours; he may buy a generator to provide electricity for them; or he may buy a television and charge them for watching it.

The most hopeful sign of all is that the children of fathers who have found only occasional employment on building sites, and of mothers who have sold things from stalls by the roadside, are moving into skilled and semi-professional jobs. This is not a process that occurs naturally. It has to be stimulated by schools and training centres that the barriadas cannot themselves provide. In the case of El Agustino, the Sons of Mary try to provide them. They do not, of course, claim to help all the children on the hill, for of a population of 200,000, well over half are under the age of 17. But they assist a good number, and, with Oxfam's support, they will soon be assisting some more. From the roof of a secondary school built at the foot of El Agustino, Brother Carbone pointed out the foundations of a new trade school. It will cost Oxfam £5,000.

For the Sons of Mary, this school is part of a broader programme of welfare and education. Their clinic, for instance, also supplied by Oxfam, is the only place where the people of El Agustino can receive medical attention without travelling to crowded hospitals in the city. There, too, they conduct a discreet family planning service, discreet because the method they encourage is sanctioned neither by the Peruvian Government nor by their Church. Six hundred lactating women are at present taking contraceptive pills under the clinic's guidance.

Its staff dispenses as much advice as medicine. Brother Carbone singled out one achievement: as a result of constant badgering, he said, local people were now boiling dirty water before drinking it. There had also been a failure. A few years ago the Sons of Mary found the money to build an incinerator. Travelling around the hill, I can appreciate their reasoning. Some of the local leaders were enthusiastic, too. The incinerator was built, but it stands idle to this day. Perhaps the people of El Agustino prefer a prospect of garbage.

The newer barriadas are further from the city. On Lima's northern extremity, 15 miles by road from the centre, there is Collique. Two years ago Collique was just a stony valley: now it supports a population of 50,000. Twenty-five miles to the south is Pamplona Alta. That was first settled as long ago as 1965. It now has a population of 30,000.

In most respects, the people have benefited by moving from town. It is healthier, land is cheap – in Pamplona Alta, where there was no invasion, it was just over £6 for a plot – and there is room to expand. There are, however, problems. The people who have jobs in Lima are miles from their work, and although public transport is excellent, the cost is a burden. Food and household goods are also, by a sad irony, more expensive in these barriadas than in town. For transportation rates are higher, and there is no refrigeration in the local shops. Moreover people who work all day – or wait for work all day – cannot afford the time to shop in the cheap central markets or respond to advertised bargains in the newspapers. Many of them cannot read them anyway.

Let us take a closer look at one section of Pamplona Alta. It is called San Francisco de la Cruz after a huge wooden cross stuck on the hilltop behind it, and has a population of 4,000. There is a certain monotony about the jobs its people do: domestic service for the women, and the building or retailing trade for the men. But monotony is better than no work at all, and half the adults of San Francisco are out of work. That includes its elected president, Señor Ernesto Franco, who showed me round one Sunday morning.

Despite a name that suggests a lengthy Spanish pedigree, Señor Franco is a mestizo, that is part Indian and part European. His biography is by no means typical of the privations that some Peruvian migrants have borne, but is a reminder of how the barriadas came to be populated. One of 12 children, he was born and had six years of schooling at a mountain town to the south. When he was 13, his father lost all his land through a lawsuit. The family had either to migrate or to starve. They chose to do the first, and came to Lima where father deposited his children in the central slum of La Victoria and went to find work. Fortunately for them, he got a job in a saw mill in the country, and was able to support Ernesto and his brothers and sisters in school. But La Victoria is not the best place to bring up a family, and when Ernesto himself married, he moved with other residents to San Francisco.

Like the people of El Agustino they have built the place

87

themselves. When I was there, 40 volunteer labourers were working on a new community centre. And families which had not sent an able-bodied man – or woman – to help the effort, had brought along food and drink for the workers. They did not lack for stimulants. From a public address system rigged up in the old community centre – a coconut matting affair – there were broadcasts of music, poetry readings, and the latest news on the World Cup.

This community centre will house a library, a clinic, an assembly room, and a workshop for the production of rugs and leather goods. It is one of four that Accion Communitaria, a Peruvian group financed by local and foreign business interests, is building in the area. Accion Communitaria supplies the materials, and the people provide the labour. Already it has made loans for the looms required for rug making, what its organiser calls a 'micro-industry'. And already it has sponsored literacy classes. It was Ernesto Franco, himself a man lucky enough to have been educated, who told me that three-quarters of the adults in San Francisco were illiterate, and added that one woman of 78 was now learning to read and write.

In the case of the Community Centre at Pamplona Alta, however, Accion Communitaria was short of funds. There are minutely-accounted limits to the philanthropy of Peruvian businessmen. So the organisation appealed to Oxfam, and Oxfam gave a minutely-accounted £5,270.

6 National Effort

'Don't talk to us about Kipling. His "great grey-green, greasy Limpopo" ran for just ten days this year.'

Scottish Agriculturalist in Botswana

Botswana has had a dreadful development decade. Estimates of the number of cattle lost through drought between 1961 and 1965 vary from a conservative 200,000 to 400,000, or a third of the national herd. Part of the difference may be accounted for in the stock that had to be rushed to the slaughterhouse before it actually died of thirst in the bush. So gloomy did the situation appear to the Department of Agriculture that in 1965 it reported: 'After four years of low rainfall and over-grazing, it seems as if the drought is becoming self-proliferating. The reflection of light and heat from the bare veld must discourage rain from falling, and it was not uncommon to see showers passing over in mid-air but not reaching the ground.'

The past five years have been a little better. More precisely, there has been one good year. During the last months of 1966 and at the beginning of 1967 it bucketed down. Twice the average rainfall was recorded in some places. The Department of Agriculture was niggardly in its gratitude: 'Communications were cut,' said the annual report, 'soils turned into a quagmire and crops rotted in the field.' In the following two years, nature was even-handed in her injustice. Rains were plentiful enough at the beginning of each season for the cattle to be watered, but poor in January and February so that the crops dried out on the stalk. To bring things up to date, the rains of 1969–70 were rotten. By May of this year, the big abattoir at Lobatse had slaughtered 30,000 more cattle than it did during the same period in 1969, a sure sign of a bad year.

This then, was Botswana's development decade. It was also her introduction to statehood. Formerly the British Protectorate of Bechuanaland, she became an independent republic in September 1966. Not a lot was going for her. She is a country two and a half times the size of the British Isles, but most of it is the infertile scrub of the Kalahari Desert. She has a population of around 650,000, of whom more than 80,000 are technically destitute – they have, that is, no observable form of income. She is also landlocked, and surrounded into the bargain by countries ranging from the black, through the unacceptable to the unmentionable – Zambia, Rhodesia, and South Africa.

Botswana pins her hopes for survival on two sectors of the economy. The first is minerals. She is already mining gold, manganese, asbestos, and kyanite in small quantities. More important, huge deposits of copper and diamonds have been discovered. The trouble here, though, is that their exploitation will be of direct benefit to no more than a few thousand of the population. Only in the longest run will a share of the royalties filter through to the counryside.

So as a people rather than as an economic unit, Botswana looks to her cattle industry. Each year it accounts for around 80 per cent of the country's exports. Some beef used to go on the hoof to Rhodesia and Zambia, but this has stopped. Now it is killed at Lobatse, and exported in a variety of forms to a number of markets. South Africa takes carcasses, as do Zambia and Swaziland. The United Kingdom last year imported 2,500 tons of canned meat from Botswana for the catering trade, and weekly consignments were flown to Switzerland during the tourist season. Valuable by-products like bonemeal, horns, and hides were also sent abroad. In 1969, 93,000 cattle were slaughtered earning over £4 million for the country. By 1975 it is planned to slaughter 150,000 head of cattle each year.

That, at least, is the way the Botswana Meat Commission sees the issue. It is viewed rather differently by the animal husbandry staff at the Ministry of Agriculture. They of course want the country to prosper as well, but they are primarily in business to ensure that individual farmers make out. It is they who must equip them to take full advantage of the new markets that the Commission is finding and supplying. In a word, they have to gear unscientific cattle-ownership to a modern industry.

Before turning to the problems that confront them, let us take a look at a local Tswana herd. By no means does it fit one's notion of cattle in the less favoured parts of the world. To the layman they appear robust and healthy. They are certainly inured to the harsh climate, and only the severest drought will drag them down. There are programmes in Botswana to cross-breed them with other strains to improve the stock, and in some places entirely foreign herds have been introduced. But experts assured me that the Tswana was an admirable breed as it was. What is more, it responds miraculously to good management.

Strictly speaking, there are few entirely traditional cattle farmers left in Botswana. Animals are not kept to provide a mangy bride price for a farmer's daughter, as happens in other parts of Africa, nor are they always retained until they die as a symbol of a farmer's status. Successive droughts and a ready market for beef have seen to that. Nevertheless they are kept too long. A Danish agriculturalist told me that cattle should be sold for slaughter after two or three years. The Botswana farmer keeps them for five.

If there is one tradition that dies particularly hard, it is that rearing cattle costs nothing. They graze freely on pastures which have been owned communally by the tribe for centuries. And neither hay nor silage is prepared for them. In turn, they till the land in the planting season, and give milk. Even the herdsmen are unpaid. They are either farmers' sons or men who receive no wages other than the right to dispose of the dead animals and of the milk.

By contrast, the techniques on offer from the Ministry of Agriculture require both a departure from tribal custom and an investment of capital. Take breeding. Bulls are generally kept with their herds the whole year round. This means that there is no selection of breeding stock and that in consequence the herd does not improve. Weaning, too, is a haphazard affair. A calf will quite happily eat grass after six months, but it will also contentedly milk its mother for a year or more if allowed to. Naturally this does not harm the calf. What it does mean is that a cow bred regularly and milked by its progeny the whole time will rapidly lose condition, and, after a year or so, fail to conceive altogether. This process results in an abysmal rate of calving. Expressed statistically, Tswana cows achieve a calving rate of about 40 per cent. If the young were weaned earlier and herded separately, there is no reason why a rate of at least 80 per cent should not be reached. This, however, would involve two herdsmen instead of one, and two kraals where one was enough before.

Keeping cattle healthy is not cheap, either. They have to be vaccinated against anthrax and rinderpest, a disease that destroyed 95 per cent of herds in Southern Africa at the end of the last century. They have also to be sprayed against tick-borne diseases like red water and gall sickness. Rearing cattle for the beef trade imposes its own particular burdens. Horns, for instance, are regarded with special pride by Botswana farmers: they are also a convenient halter for tying or leading the animals. Yet an exporting industry requires them to be slaughtered and processed under rigidly controlled conditions, and they have therefore to be transported great distances by rail and road to the abattoir. Horned animals can wound themselves terribly – as well as decrease in value – on the journey. And de-horning equipment costs money.

Most important of all, farmers have to be shown how to make money out of their cattle. Castrating young bulls to improve the quality and quantity of the meat is one way. Improving their feeding is another. I have already mentioned silage and hay which are not widely used. Next there is a method for compensating various deficiencies in the dry soil of Botswana. The most serious is a lack of phosphorus which the animal needs for the proper growth of its bones. Indeed, without phosphorus, cattle will eat any rotting bone-matter that they can find, and contract botulism as a result. My dictionary describes botulism as 'sausage poisoning' which conveys the point.

Even with special feeding, livestock needs steady and assured grazing. This it rarely gets. The tribal system of communal ownership of land results not only in the indiscriminate grazing of pasture in a good year, but also in its tragic over-grazing during a bad one. Once over-grazed, land deteriorates: grass fails to grow and soil is eroded. There is a simple answer, simpler perhaps in its telling than in its execution. Tribal land has to be divided and fenced. This will enable grass to grow in a good year, and allow it to recover after a bad one. The land can then be grazed in rotation.

This introduction to animal husbandry in Botswana is essential background to one of the larger projects that Oxfam has funded for the Ministry of Agriculture. On the principle of seeing is believing, the Ministry has set up seven cattle-holding grounds in the country, one in each of the tribal areas. To these have been added demonstration herds of a bull and 20 or so heifers. The primary purpose of the holding grounds is to provide local farmers with the means of fattening up their cattle for market. They pay 7s. a month for each animal kept on the ranch, and a limit of six animals is imposed on each farmer. During their stay, the cattle are dewormed, deticked, and fed with bonemeal to overcome the lack of phosphorus in their natural diet. Each holding ground has between 4,000 and 7,000 acres of pasture which is fenced so that the grazing can be properly controlled.

No farmer is likely to be impressed by such novelties unless his purse benefits. At Morale, the ranch which serves the Bamangwato tribe and which I visited one morning, there have been a number of heavier purses. After six months of good management, cattle there put on about 200 lbs in weight; their meat, by the system used at the Lobatse abattoir, also goes up a couple of grades in quality. In terms of hard cash, this amounts to about £10 a beast, achieved for an investment of £2.

These ranches serve a no less valuable purpose as places of education. Farmers are encouraged to visit them, and to see the progress of their cattle. The demonstration herds, moreover, as well as being a source of revenue for the ranches, are a reminder of the benefits of long-term management. To give just one example, the cows are bred as regularly as they are in the bush, but with better feeding achieve a remarkable calving rate of 90 per cent. Such lessons can be particularly well taught at Morale. For just down the road is the rural training centre at Mahalapye, and farmers attending courses are regularly brought to view the herd and its achievements.

Kingsley Butler, the chief animal production officer at the Ministry, wants to attach a training centre to each demonstration ranch. For the time being he is content with the effect that the others are having on wary local leaders. The land for one ranch, which has enjoyed the same success as Morale, was given to the Ministry because, as a member of the District Council put it, 'our own cattle usually die there'.

In a country like Botswana it is not enough to set up demonstration ranches. Each serves an area no smaller than half the counties in England, and its capacity is limited to 200 cattle at a time. Although the Government itself has a network of trained agricultural demonstrators, it is often difficult to persuade them to work in the less developed parts of the country. So Oxfam has again stepped into the breach, at first tentatively and more recently with both feet. With a grant of £5,000 in 1967, the Department of Agriculture – as it was then called – established a small mobile animal husbandry unit in Ngamiland, the north-western corner of the country. In monthly tours from Maun, the biggest town in the area, a team of two gave refresher courses to agricultural demonstrators in techniques of castration, de-horning and spraying. It also contacted more remote farmers both to instruct them and to sell them bonemeal and the implements of their trade.

So well-received by farmers was this unit that the Government is considering setting up others. Oxfam has led the way. At an initial cost of £11,000, there is now a larger and better equipped team operating from Mahalapye in the East. It does not travel light. With agricultural demonstrators, equipment and feeding material on board, its trucks undertake prolonged safaris in the bush. At each water-hole an agricultural demonstrator is dropped off to work with the farmers for four or five days. When the trucks have no more demonstrators to drop, they return to pick them all up, and so proceed. When they have exhausted their supplies of bonemeal and implements (sold at above market rate so as not to discourage the retail trade) they return to Mahalapye. A cautious Kingsley Butler pointed out to me that it was too early to judge the team's success. It has, after all, been going only since last year. 'But,' he added, 'all the signs are good.'

Are the techniques propagated by the Ministry generally adopted? I am no farmer, even less am I qualified to judge developments in Botswana agriculture. So I rely on the experts. Richard Gilmour, who showed me the ranch at Morale, told me that some quite definitely were. Despite their being against tribal custom and often being resisted by District Councils, fences were being put up to control grazing. Eric Rempel, a Canadian agricultural volunteer and fluent master of his subject, was also confident of progress. He gave two examples. The advantages of castration were now recognised by farmers, he said, as was the value of a sire of quality for their cows. Figures support these contentions. Between 1964 and 1967, the number of kraals improved and built each year rose from 37 to 242. During the same period the number of cattle castrated increased from 2,197 to 10,756, and while at the beginning only 1,280 farmers bought bonemeal, 9,179 were buying it by 1967.

That is one question. Here is another. Could Tswana cattle survive another drought of the severity they experienced – and to which so many succumbed – in the first years of the sixties? Any improvement in their general condition would doubtless contribute to their survival. But more than that, they need water, and they need permanent supplies of it.

The exigencies of the Botswana climate have forced cattle and their herdsmen to be migratory. The annual cycle runs like this. During the rainy season (November to February) animals are watered at the rivers in the east. These never flow throughout the year, and in a bad year the smaller ones do not flow at all. Last year the sizable Mahalapye river earned its name on only two days. Nevertheless even flash floods leave pools behind them where livestock can drink. And when they do not, there is water in the sandy river beds that can be fairly easily extracted.

In March, when this source has dried up, cattle are moved 30 or 40 miles to the west where natural pans maintain them until the rains come in November. Again, in a bad year, this does not happen. At the height of the last drought, cattle had to trek huge distances to find water, some of them drinking only every third day. And this had a more alarming effect than is immediately apparent. For the land surrounding pans that held water was greatly overgrazed, and in some cases the damage is permanent.

In most parts of the country there is no source of underground water. So well-boring is impracticable. Only one solution remains: dams have to be built to store the rains artificially. Some, of course, existed before the big drought. Indeed three Oxfam grants, made each year from 1963 to 1965 and amounting in all to £35,000, went as much on repairing old dams as on building new ones. They served the additional purpose of providing paid employment in areas where farmers had temporarily lost their livelihood. After the drought a scheme was drawn up by the UK Freedom from Hunger Committee to tackle the problem on a far wider scale. It involved the establishment of a soil conservation and mobile dam building unit, the cost of which was just under £166,000. It was met jointly by Oxfam and Christian Aid.

This unit, which by May 1969, had built 25 large dams, has spawned yet another, more modest enterprise. Called the small dam construction unit, it has forsaken one of the objectives of the original programme which was to employ as little machinery and as much local labour as possible. The new unit has a Crawler tractor and a bulldozer with its earth-moving accoutrements, all funded by Oxfam. It is always best, as Oxfam recognises, to involve a community – preferably on a voluntary basis – in work that is being done for its own benefit. David Swart, the South African civil engineer who runs the dam-building unit, told me that the villagers are supposed to fence in the new dams and plant grass around them as their contribution to the scheme. But this they rarely do.

One afternoon in May I accompanied Swart on a tour of the area in which the unit was working. We encountered it near Oodi, a village about 30 miles north of Gaborone, the tiny Botswana capital. Oodi is picturesquely sited below a rank of lumpy black hills, but there is no water for miles. 'God knows,' Swart remarked as he passed through it, 'why they built a village here.' But they did, and they need water: at present the nearest permanent supply for their animals is at Mochudi, 15 miles away. The unit will not take long to provide it. Foreman Morgan, a cheerful character from up-country Botswana in pink sun hat and boiler suit, had had his gang on the Oodi dam for a month. Already the earth barrier had been thrown up, and the bulldozer was clearing the floor of the dam of its trees and boulders. Another month, said Morgan, and they would be through. Oodi could then look forward to the rains, and even to the following dry season.

During the afternoon I saw five of the 15 dams that the unit had built or repaired in the previous 14 months. They cover an area of 500 square miles and a cattle population of 6,800. Each dam should support no more than 400 head of cattle, and its purpose is not simply to water them. 'We are in business,' Swart said, 'to improve these animals.'

His reasoning is straightforward. If cattle are given a permanent drinking supply, then they will not have to wander the bush looking for water. And if enough small dams are constructed to support all the cattle in the region, then farmers can afford to use the grazing land around them sparingly. A sedentary cattle population has another advantage: agricultural extension workers will be able more easily to reach and advise the farmers. Well-sited dams bring, too, a host of benefits to the villagers themselves. Swart says that he regularly adjusts to appeals from villagers for drinking water. At Morwa, for instance, the new dam above the village had replaced an old one below it. 'All the muck from Morwa used to drain into that one,' Swart observed with a grimace.

In Botswana there are numerous small cattle-owners who will benefit from the schemes I have described. But it is as well to remember that 40 per cent of the country's livestock is owned by 5 per cent of the people; more glaringly, 10 per cent of the people own 90 per cent of the cattle. Swart told me a story that illustrates the point nicely. Inspecting a dam one day, he was approached by a grubby and dishevelled old farmer who began plying him with questions about cattle disease. He told Swart he was worried to death about his animals. Though no agriculturalist, Swart was brought up on a farm in South Africa, and is fluent in Setswana, the local language. He did his best to answer the old man's questions, and agreed to accompany him to inspect the herd. When they arrived at the cattle post, he saw 900 head before him. 'There he was,' said Swart, 'eating out of my hand, and he could have bought me out nine times over.'

This creates a difficulty for Oxfam. Quite rightly, their policy is to help the small farmer, not the man who could buy out a well-paid civil engineer nine times over. In Botswana, it is a particular dilemma because to provide water in an area is to benefit both the rich and the poor. For me it was resolved by every expert I met. Interviews always returned to the terrifying destruction of the great drought. 'Remember,' said Swart, 'a quarter of a million cattle died in those years.'

What, though, has Oxfam done for the farmer who has no cattle at all, the farmer who each year must spite the climate by growing crops to feed his family?

One answer is provided in the rural training centre at Mahalapye. Expanded with Oxfam money to enable almost 1,000 to attend short courses each year, it is one of two in the country. They both exist for the same purpose: to raise standards in all aspects of rural life. Farmers are instructed in relatively simple techniques like cultivating in rows and ploughing before the rains. This so-called winter-ploughing is of value because it ensures that moisture seeps into the ground, and does not run off the hard, sun-baked crust.

At Mahalapye there is a splendid market garden, a regular flowering desert which is irrigated by waste water from the huts used by student-farmers. Here they are introduced to vegetables that, with luck and perseverance by their instructors, they can grow on their farms. Here also are rabbits, unheard of in rural Botswana, and chickens, which are regarded with suspicion as eggs are popularly supposed to affect one's fertility, and well-groomed pigs. The Botswana pig is a peculiarly ill-favoured creature which runs around the village picking up all manner of things, not least a number of distasteful diseases. To establish the contrast, a fine porker is slaughtered on each course at Mahalapye, and eaten by the student farmers.

When I was visiting Oodi, I happened to meet a farmer who had attended one of these courses. His name was Mr T. N. Molwantwa, and he was headmaster of the local primary school. Looking at my notebook, he said, 'I'm very game to talk to you fellows,' and another interview began. Mr Molwantwa was rather grander than most of the people in Oodi: he owned 28 acres, and the average holding was 12. He was also the only villager who had had a course at a rural training centre. It showed.

He was now ploughing during winter to prepare the soil for his sorghum, millet, and beans. Only one other farmer in Oodi was doing the same. His 13 cattle had benefited, too. He was now spraying them against ticks, and had dug a silage pit for their feeding. On the advice of his instructor, he had built a cattle crush, and bought a de-horning iron. How long had it taken him to learn these things? 'It was a week's course,' said Mr Molwantwa, and hurried back to his schoolroom.

The rural training centres have duties other than helping farmers. First they give refresher courses to agricultural demonstrators. These days Botswana demonstrators are graduating from the posh new agricultural college near Gadborone. But when the extension service began in Bechuanaland in the fifties, there was no such institution. For qualified demonstrators the country looked to Africans from neighbouring Rhodesia and South Africa, men who were only too anxious to leave. The Ministry of Agriculture still relies heavily upon them.

Courses are also held for the women. They are given classes on nutrition, child care, hygiene in the home, cooking, and gardening. And that is not all. For the rural training centres promise to range over almost every activity known to the countryside. Butchers and shop-owners come for instruction, as do tractor-owners. There need not be many courses for the latter: at the last count there were 655 tractors in Botswana. And at Mahalapye there was recently a course for police officers on explosives. As the mining industry develops, not all of its contrivances will remain in safe hands. The centres award a simple, but fetching diploma. Wilson McKinlay, the Scottish principal of the Mahalapye centre, told me that he had found them in homes in the remotest parts of the bush. Elaborately framed, they were invariably the only decoration on the walls.

Botswana, however, faces a more urgent educational problem than can be solved by rural training centres. It lies in the schools themselves, and is shared by many developing countries. Inspired by the worthiest of motives, governments have given priority to building schools on the pattern of our own in the West. Colonial administrations, they complain, conspicuously neglected to pursue the ideal of universal education. They were right. What they did not appear to grasp was that universal education can be afforded only by highly developed countries.

Without an economy advanced enough to absorb qualified young people, education serves merely to dissatisfy them with the life that their fathers have led, and puts nothing in its place. In India, for instance, vast numbers of university graduates cannot find employment. In the Sudan, graduates regularly riot against their Government for not giving them jobs. Too late, new governments have realised that education must proceed in step with their countries' development.

In Botswana there is no problem with university graduates because the country has only just begun to build its first university campus. The difficulty occurs further down the line in the primary schools. There are over 250 of these, and just ten or so secondary schools. Thus no more than a fifth of primary school leavers stand to gain a place in a secondary school. The answer is not, as may be supposed, to increase the number of secondary schools. For that would merely shelve the problem for a few years. Nor is it necessary to reduce the number of primary schools. What has to be done is to gear education more to practicalities and less to academic pursuits, and also to pick up the casualties of what the Botswana Government now calls the 'primary school leaver problem'.

Meet Julius. He lives in Mochudi, this straggling town of 17,000 in south eastern Botswana. There are five primary schools in Mochudi, from one of which Julius has a leaving certificate. He started school late, however, and was 17 when he left after seven years of education. That meant that he was too old to go to one of the two secondary schools in the town. He was also, he admits, not particularly qualified to do anything else. So what options were there open to him? 'Well,' he said with that precise and imaginative use of our language that only foreigners seem to achieve. 'I could have lingered in the village.' Then he thought, and added with an uncomfortable grin: 'Or I could have gone to the mines.'

When the people of Botswana talk to you about 'the mines', they are not referring to their own new mining industry. They mean the South African mines where thousands of their countrymen are employed. It is not slavery: the correct phrase, I believe, is 'indentured labour'. Julius could have signed up with any of three recruiting offices in Mochudi on either a six-month or a nine-month contract. He would then have been given free travel to Johannesburg, and earned 4s. 6d. a day shovelling waste material into trucks underground. Had he taken a nine-month contract, he would have returned to Mochudi the richer by £40.

Instead of taking up that option, Julius joined 30 other young men on the builders' brigade attached to the community development centre at Mochudi. The centre began in 1963 to receive and resettle African refugees from South Africa, and now seeks to alleviate the problems of primary school leavers in the district. Run by a burly and forceful UNA worker who is blessed with the name of Ian Smith, it has a finger in every pie. As well as the builders' brigade, there is a night school, built of course by the builders, a leather workshop, an excellent little newspaper called *The Voice*, a market garden, and a training scheme for motor mechanics. Oxfam's contribution to the centre itself is to pay part of Smith's salary.

Although not the leader of the building team, Julius is recognised as its best bricklayer. Smith predicted that eight of the 12 trainees who were to finish this year would pass their trades test, and that Julius would come out top. He should not find it difficult to get work. In Gaborone, where a lot of new building is going up, a bricklayer's income can be as high as £50 a month. And there are other opportunities in the traditional sector of the industry. At any rate, Julius told me he was aiming at a wage of £20 a month at the beginning, or an hourly rate of about 5s.,* a little more, that is, than he could earn in a South African mine in a day.

Leaving Julius and his colleagues at work in Mochudi, I drove north by landrover to Nfetledi. It is a journey of some 70 miles, memorable only for the termite hills that stand guard over the bush like sentry boxes. At Nfetledi Linchwe II, chief of the Bakgatla tribe, has some arable land and a cattle post. One of the youngest and most progressive of the chiefs, Linchwe has long been associated with the centre at Mochudi, his tribe's main town. But now that he is Botswana's Ambassador to the United States, he has no need for the present of his land and his cattle. So they are on loan to the centre as a training ground for some of his young tribesmen.

David Mokgatlhane comes from a village 30 miles south of Mochudi, and has been at Nfetledi for almost two years. He, like Julius, has had seven years of primary education, and 12 months at the night school in Mochudi as well. Unlike Julius, however, he wants to be a farmer. This was no soft option. Indeed, without land of his own, without machinery and

* These figures, I realise, are not consistent. That is Julius's problem.

without capital, it was, with the exception of the mines, the hardest option of all. He could have joined the builders in Mochudi, and eventually traded his skills for a regular wage. Or he could have applied to the Botswana Agricultural College and, if accepted, looked forward to a fat salary as a demonstrator. But David prefers to be his own boss, and, with what he has learnt at Nfetledi, he is confident that he can make a good living from the land. In his diffident way, David is hugely ambitious.

His father has 40 cattle and 30 acres of land. According to David, he is not much of a farmer. 'He only grows to eat,' says David a little disdainfully. When he returns to his family after two years' training, he is going to change all that. First he will look after his father's cattle, and then in five years or so he will go to his local chief and ask for some land. This he will clear to make new fields and establish a vegetable garden. And David has already shown that farmer's instinct for saving and investment which is sometimes mistaken for miserliness. With his pocket money of 5s. a week, he has bought ten goats in the last 20 months at about £2 a head. If my arithmetic is correct, that left precious little in his pocket.

David and nine other young farmers are being trained at Nfetledi by Eric Rempel, a Mennonite volunteer from Manitoba, Canada. The Mennonite sect, was, I confess, a new one on me. Perhaps both groups will forgive me if I describe it – for the benefit of the similarly ignorant – as a sect that has much in common with the Quakers.

Rempel has a degree in agriculture from the University of Manitoba, and has worked on the training programme since it started in 1969. He lives in a rondavel no more pretentious than those occupied by his students, and says that after a three-week stint in the bush he can speak only pidgin English. He is maintained there by Oxfam which also provided everything else for the project from breeding stock to toolsheds. It is costing £16,800.

When I visited the project, Rempel's standing among his students could scarcely have been higher. With their help he had achieved the near impossible, or at least something that no farmer within a 20-mile radius of Nfetledi had achieved. After a planting and growing season of abysmally bad rains, he had harvested a respectable crop.

In fact, he had harvested a number of crops. Each student is given eight acres, and told to plant them with four of the following – sorghum, beans, groundnuts, millet, maize, and sunflowers. Some of the produce is eaten on the project; the rest is sold. Sunflower seeds, for instance, are used in the manufacture of cooking oil in South Africa. But on all of them the students have to keep proper accounts of expenditure and income. The profit is divided: three-quarters of it covers the overheads of the training programme, and the students keep the remaining quarter. This year there will be a reasonable profit.

Rempel is no magician; he even makes a point of avoiding the use of sophisticated farm machinery. True, he gives his students some training on an old tractor once in a while. But this, he says, is just to boost their ego: 'It's really quite unrealistic. Unless a young farmer is very rich, it will take him 30 or 40 years to save for a tractor.' Rempel's results this year were more the product of those techniques of winter ploughing and planting in rows. There is simply no other way. Rempel told me of what happens when they are not used: 'Farmers get tremendously enthusiastic at the beginning of the rains. "Come and plough, come and plough," they say. After two months, nothing. The old way was quite profitable in the fifties when the rains were decent, but it just doesn't work now.'

David and Julius are, if you like, two casualties of the educational system in Botswana. They have been helped. The sensible way to solve the problem, though, would be to change the system. I am not suggesting one of those rosy 'back-to-the-land' movements, rather the re-equipping of schools to face eventualities for their pupils other than an office desk. In some measure, this is already happening. Agricultural studies are now a part of the primary school syllabus, and a few more advanced institutions have put 'Development Studies' on their timetables. If one wants to locate the origin of this revolution, one must drive north from Nfetledi for about 150 miles, turn off the main road outside Palapye, and visit the Swaneng Hill School near Serowe.

To have spent just one afternoon at Swaneng was to do it the scantest of justice. One incident, however, may convey the flavour of the place. I arrived in the middle of one of those crises which periodically reverberate through secondary schools. But the nature of Swaneng's crisis was novel. The fifth form academic boys were apparently protesting at having to do 'community work', a stilted euphemism in this case for digging a trench for a new electricity cable. The founder and principal of the school, Patrick van Rensburg, had accordingly got up in the middle of the night, gone to their form-room and scrawled 'ELITIST' across the blackboard.

Elitism and the temptation to divorce school life from that of the community in which it is set are things that Swaneng has combated since it began in 1963. The first buildings, as an example, were built by the first students; every boy must attend classes on building, woodwork, and dam construction; every girl is taught dressmaking, crafts, gardening, and cooking. As it has grown, with the help of Oxfam and other agencies, the school has evolved the more specialised concept of 'brigade training'. This military phrase denotes nothing more violent than that teams of trainees should by their own production cover the running costs of their courses. At Swaneng there is a builders' brigade, a mechanical brigade, a farmers' brigade, a tanning brigade, and a women's textile brigade.

The farmers' brigade, which can accommodate up to 120 primary school leavers at a time, has been set up with a grant of £50,000 from the Danish Government. It appears to have everything. But Vernon Gibberd, the Englishman who runs it and whose salary is paid by Oxfam, admits to a problem. Originally it was planned that the trainees should be resettled in co-operative groups on tribal lands: local tribal leaders seem to have thought otherwise. So the students will have a difficult time of it adjusting from the relatively sophisticated, even elitist, life at Swaneng to more rugged conditions at home. For the next batch, Gibberd is determined to ensure that there are better facilities for his farmers after training.

In the meantime, these issues had evidently escaped a young man called Ditshwanelo whom I met in the brigade's vegetable garden. He was quite confident that he could make out as a market gardener, and displayed customary impatience with the older generation of Botswana farmers. 'They are unskilled,' he said. 'I do not know how they will ever develop the country.'

From Swaneng back to Gaborone takes five hours by landrover. For most of the journey, one follows a railway line which links Bulawayo, in Rhodesia, with Mafeking, in South Africa. And the engines and the rolling stock one sees on that line have 'Rhodesian Railways' marked quite clearly upon them. Moreover, the faces which gaze from the cabs of these engines are distinctly white. The sceptical traveller may be forgiven for feeling that it is a trifle odd to see white men driving Rhodesian trains through independent black Africa.

Botswana's leaders acknowledge the anomaly, but can do nothing to resolve it. For as well as providing Rhodesia with a supply-route, the railway is also Botswana's lifeline. It carries her cattle to the abattoir at Lobatse and on to Johannesburg as beef, it brings her milk from Rhodesia, and most of her other imports from South Africa.

Some development agencies, on the other hand, choose to ignore Botswana's predicament, and stipulate that she should not use their money to trade with her southern neighbours. Though splendidly liberal, this is a nonsense. It means first that any item of aid must be imported at vast expense from acceptable countries in the West, instead of coming from South Africa where it is also likely to be manufactured. In turn this means that Botswana does not gain the cash value of such an investment. And thirdly, it means that the country is denied the excellent technical services of South African industry and commerce. Even the radicals I met in Botswana recognised that their country would gain economic independence of South Africa only by accepting South African services for the time being.

Oxfam imposes no such terms on its aid to Botswana. Before howls of protest are raised at the fact, let us examine how this policy works in practice. A few years ago Oxfam made 100 loans of £250 each to farmers who wanted to drill bore-holes to water their livestock. It was a success. The bore-holes were constructed – with South African equipment and materials – and the loans repaid. Had the equipment been imported from outside South Africa the loans required would have been far larger. Most of the farmers could not have afforded the repayments.

*

During the sixties Oxfam has given around £$\frac{1}{2}$ million to Botswana. By contrast, the British Government last year gave the country more than £1 million in development grants alone. The difference is striking. No less striking is the way in which the two bodies have spent their money. For 'development' covers activities that range from building office blocks for civil servants to helping a farmer to grow better crops. Roger Slade, of the Government's Division of Planning and Statistics, put the contrast succinctly: 'The whole of Gaborone was built with British money. But out in the country a farmer tilling his field knows about Oxfam.'

This was not the only tribute that was paid to Oxfam during my visit. Indeed, I was burdened with them. Ian Smith at Mochudi, for instance, compared Oxfam's approach to that of some other private aid agencies: 'They're just looking for the quick tear. Oxfam is streets ahead – the only one with any sense as far as I'm concerned.' Back at the Ministry of Agriculture, Brian Batwell, director of Agricultural Extension, told me that without Oxfam's help, 'there would probably be no rural training centres in the country today'. The sceptic here may take refuge in the suggestion that if Oxfam had not helped, then someone else would have done. But in Botswana even that comfortable notion is denied him. The mobile animal husbandry project was turned down by several other agencies.

In the view of Kingsley Butler, chief animal production officer in the Ministry, there was virtually no agricultural extension work done in Botswana until Oxfam arrived. 'Without that first grant for our animal husbandry services,' he told me, 'I don't know what would have happened.' To my mind, it is a sufficient achievement to have helped a few poor farmers with a grant of a few pounds. At the cost of £$\frac{1}{2}$ million in Botswana, Oxfam has helped a whole country. That is an achievement of a very different order.

7 Missionaries in Development

'If the Americans would send fertiliser and not food,
then these people could grow their own food. But
the Americans don't have a surplus of fertiliser.'

Father Tryers

There is something symbolic in the way the Dagomba tribe
of northern Ghana bury their dead. It is also a little dis-
criminatory. A male corpse is laid facing the east so that when
he sees the sun rising in the after-life, he will know it is time
to go to work in the fields. A female corpse, on the other hand,
is buried facing the west. As the sun begins to drop towards
the horizon, she will know that it is time to collect her pots
and go to fetch the water. For that, more or less, is the pattern
of rural life in northern Ghana.

I know little more of what the Dagomba tribesman believes
will happen to him after death. For his sake I hope only that
water is in more plentiful supply there than it is here on
earth. For five months in the year the villages around Tamale,
the capital of northern Ghana, are bone dry. That, admittedly,
is not entirely the fault of nature. The rains that begin in
May and June, and continue more heavily during July,
August, and September can produce as much as 67 inches in a
good year, or as little as 30 inches in a poor one. Either way,
not enough is done to conserve it, and come February and
March the situation is annually critical.

Father Milette, a French-Canadian priest, knows an old
character in one village who, as a young man, had to send his
womenfolk 20 miles to fetch water. That has changed: now
the most they have to walk is five miles. Think of that,
though: five miles every day during each dry season, two and
a half of them balancing four to five gallons on your head.
And it is not only the wives and the grandmothers who turn
out. Little girls with pot bellies and strings of beads around

their midriffs carry little calabashes, bigger girls with more clothes carry clay pots, and in front of them all marches mother with a huge tin drum. And where are they going? Not, to be sure, to a clear spring or a clean tap. If they are lucky, they will find water in a decently covered well. If the well has dried up, they will find it in an open hole in the ground. The water there will be the colour and the consistency of runny custard, and the women will compete for it with their cattle, their sheep, and their goats.

When they get this mixture back to their compounds, it will neither be boiled nor filtered. Indeed the very suggestion often provokes amusement. So it is drunk as it is, and the results are everywhere apparent. I asked Father Milette about guinea worms as we stood on the bank of one of these muddy little reservoirs. He pointed to a boy next to us, and asked his mother to bring the child closer. But the boy resisted, and began to scream. That amused everyone, too. It did not really matter. Even at a few yards one could see the tiny gashes where worms had been wound from his limbs on a twig. Guinea worms, Father explained, live by their thousand in this water. Straining it through a handkerchief is enough to remove them.

Following Father Milette and his young Spanish colleague, Father Estaban, I walked from the reservoir into one of the villages. We had to pay our respects to the local sub-chief. As we approached through a crowd of excited children, a boy brought his little brother for Father Estaban to see. His hairless head was covered in sticky, sickly boils. 'Father,' began the older boy, and then reverted to the local dialect. 'What did you tell him,' I asked Estaban when the brothers had run off? 'I told him to get his mother to scrub it with soap and water, but it's malnutrition, really. I usually bring some vitamins with me. You see, there's no Government clinic or Government dispensary round here. Vitamins, that's my bible.' By now the crowd was pressing on us once more. 'Look,' said Father Estaban, 'more malnutrition,' and he stopped to greet another child. His hair was a sandy ginger in colour instead of black, and Estaban could pull it out in tufts.

The chief's compound was the same as all the others – a group of single-roomed mud huts around a central space for cooking. At night some of them would be occupied by animals, others by the women and one would be set aside for the chief. There was a special hut for receiving guests, too. This one had bits of broken china stuck around the door by way of decoration. Here we paid our respects.

No woman, of course, dared intrude on such an important meeting, but as we rose to go a girl entered from the compound with a baby at her breast. It was her first child, and an ailing little thing at that. Large and lustreless eyes stared wanly around it, its ribs were visibly corrugated, and the muscles of its legs and arms were puffy and powerless. 'Malnutrition,' said Father Estaban for the third time in a quarter of an hour. Then the chief rummaged around at the back of the hut, and found a bag of eggs to present to me. 'Wouldn't it be better if . . .', I began to say to Father Milette. 'No,' he replied before I could finish, 'it would be very rude not to accept them. Eggs are always being given as gifts here. We get a lot of them.' It would surprise no one, least of all the villagers themselves, if that baby was now dead. About half the children born around Tamale die before they are four.

There is no war going on in northern Ghana. Nor has there been any influx of refugees to use up its resources. What I have described is the general and immemorial conditions of its people.

Aid has come in the past to northern Ghana. Indeed, during the Nkrumah regime, it came thick and fast. The big idea then was State farms which would employ hundreds, and make the north not only self-sufficient, but also enable it to export its grain.

Money and machinery, however, do not necessarily add up to development, and the State farms failed. The causes of their failure were manifold: their managers were chosen as much for political reasons as for their agricultural qualifications, spares were in short supply, and above all the idea lost favour as rapidly as did Nkrumah. The results of this failure are visible around Tamale: parks of rusting farm machinery from harrows and tractors, to bulldozers and combine harvesters. In one of them I saw twelve Russian snow-ploughs, an inappropriate gift to tropical Africa. And in Tamale itself, there is a more recent example of how a well-financed and ambitious enterprise can work against the interests of the poor. An Italian company has built a bright new factory to make Pito, the local beer. With this single gesture they have removed the livelihood of the women who traditionally make the stuff in their huts.

If they had the money, the White Fathers in Tamale could be more ambitious. But they would ensure, I suspect, that the people, not the State and the private entrepreneurs, were the beneficiaries. Their mission started in the town in 1946, and since that time they have worked gradually outwards to serve the rural population. While at the beginning they ministered to the Roman Catholic southerners who had come to Tamale as civil servants or traders, their work now is with the Moslem – or at least Moslemised – people of the countryside.

That Christian Missionaries should be helping Moslem villagers might strike the layman as at best curious and at worst meddlesome. But that would be to misunderstand the White Fathers. Sitting at lunch one day with the Bishop of Tamale and some of the fathers, I asked whether they regarded themselves primarily as proselytizers of their faith. The Bishop replied benignly: 'No, we are here to help.' Less benignly, one father produced an imaginary gun from under the table, and shot me with great deliberation through the heart.

The help that the White Fathers bring used to be seen only in the schools they manage in the town and out in the bush. They are, as one put it, the 'unpaid paymasters' of the Government. In other words, each school receives a grant, and it is the fathers' job to help build it, to provide desks and to keep the staff paid and happy. Now, there are more urgent priorities, and the emphasis is on agricultural schemes and the provision of water. The water needed, as we have seen, is not for tremendous irrigation works, but simply for drinking. The Bishop told me of an occasion recently when an agriculturalist inquired whether he would support a campaign to introduce kitchen gardens around Tamale: 'He asked me why I was laughing. I said I hadn't had a drop of water in the house for ten days. You can't have kitchen gardens without water.'

Before the White Fathers brought a reservoir to Chirifoyili last year, they were already well-known in the area. It was not like those first exploratory tours of the diocese in the late forties: at that time screaming women and crying children left their pots and their animals at the approach of such strange figures, and fled into the bush. Near Chirifoyili the White Fathers had already built a school, a dispensary, and a chapel. It was as well they thought of the chapel. Its vestry doubles as the dispensary, and since the school's tin roof blew off in a gale the other day, its nave has done service as a classroom.

Work on the reservoir began in March 1969, and was completed in a couple of months. Two Government bulldozers were hired out, and their cost was split between Oxfam and the people who expected to benefit. Each compound from the 13 villages around Chirifoyili contributed a little under £5 to the scheme. The new reservoir was not without its problems. At the beginning there was a considerable loss of water through seepage, something the villagers attributed to the White Fathers' failure to placate their land god. But now it holds its water well, and when I saw it at the end of the dry season was a good five feet deep.

There can be no doubt of the value of this scheme. Though impure, the water is within easier reach of the villages than their previous supply for the dry season. Women from the most distant village now have to walk only two and a half miles to the new reservoir.

But it does not satisfy Father Tryers. He regards dams and reservoirs as a stop-gap, something that will ensure the people's survival, but not their progress. On this last theme he will expatiate brilliantly for hours.

His views are based on 20 years of acute observation of the Ghanaian scene. He has also lived through some harsh times himself. Born and brought up in central Liverpool during the depression, he was ordained a White Father in North Africa at the beginning of the last war. When the area was overrun by the Germans, he escaped by walking through the enemy lines disguised as an Arab. This was easily done. A White Father's vestments are modelled on Arab dress; the only addition is a rosary.

All civilisation, Father Tryers argues, stems from leisure. In particular, no society has flourished without a degree of female emancipation. Women should have the time and the energy to devote to bringing up their children; in an ideal world, too, their daughters should receive as much education as their sons so that in time they will be able to impart this knowledge to their own children. In the villages around

111

Tamale this is indeed a revolutionary doctrine. The women here are child-bearing and water-carrying drudges. 'There will be no betterment in the north,' says Father Tryers, 'until there is water on every doorstep.' He sometimes puts this point to men in the villages. They know him well, and they love him dearly, but they also laugh at him. Women, they say, have always walked miles for water.

Father Tryers explained his idea to me as we trudged from well to water-hole and from water-hole to well in the bush that surrounds Cheshe, a village five miles from Tamale. There the White Fathers are sinking five new wells. The digging, a skilled and at times dangerous job, is being done by the local council which is also paying a small labour force from the village to cart away the earth. The villagers are themselves paying about £10 for each well, and Oxfam has made a small grant to cover the cost of the cementing.

Father Tryers is not at all happy with the scheme. The return on all this effort, he says, is pitiful. It certainly seemed so to me. When water is struck, it is in yellow dribbles, not in clear torrents. And sometimes the well-diggers dynamite their way through rock to find no moisture at all underneath. What Tryers proposes is that each compound should have its own catchment tank. 'You have to realise first,' he says, 'that the ground water here is not worth bothering over. Only the very best well does not dry up, and bore-holes are out.'

Government schemes for small dams are little better: 'They dry up through evaporation and seepage. And besides, when the rains come, every foul disease you can think of is washed down into them from their banks.' Tanks have the virtue of utter simplicity – 'It's the simple ideas we want,' says Father Tryers. They are also cheap to build. All that is required is a hole in the ground, large enough to retain a compound's water supply for the dry season. It should be lined with polythene to prevent seepage, and covered with branches and earth to prevent evaporation. A good storm, Tryers reckons, would fill one in half an hour.

That villagers should eventually tumble to this idea is not a forlorn hope. In some compounds there are already crudely-constructed tanks which provide unseasonal water for building and repairing the huts. That they should build similar structures for their own comfort and for the advance of their womenfolk is a novel suggestion, but one that with Father Tryers's dogmatic insistence might one day catch on.

If Tryers is a convincing champion of the necessity for social change in the Tamale diocese, he also yields to no one in his criticism of the big development schemes that the diocese has seen. For State farms, he would substitute village co-operatives. 'We must,' he says, 'get these huge enterprises out of our head.'

Effective agricultural development in the villages means that spiritual welfare can no longer take pride of place for the White Fathers. In Cheshe, for instance, there is a community of 17 adult Christians as well as a number of children under instruction. Just a few years ago, the catechist appointed by the White Fathers to look after the village would have been neither a native of Cheshe nor in any other way connected with its economic life. Now he is both a resident and a farmer. And his first Christian duty will be to start a co-operative in the village to farm 200 acres of rice.

Of all the big projects to start in northern Ghana since the war, none was more ambitious than the Gonja Development Corporation at Damongo, 80 miles from Tamale. Modelled on the East African Groundnuts Scheme, of sacred memory, it put 3,000 or 4,000 acres under cultivation, built houses and sheds, and equipped a hospital to serve its expatriate and Ghanaian workers. But like its more notorious predecessor, it was also a most resounding flop. When it was finally wound up during the fifties, most of its cultivated land reverted to tangled bush, its houses and sheds were boarded up and the hospital was left to decay.

In part, it still resembles a wartime aerodrome. But a full 1,000 acres have been acquired by the White Fathers, and they are not the sort of people to let the bush grow under their feet.

By tradition the Gonja people who inhabit the bush around Damongo are hunters. So the agricultural work of the White Fathers' mission in the town is aimed more at the densely populated and over-cultivated regions to the north, near the border with Upper Volta. Here the problem is much the same as that already encountered in Botswana: the terrific rise in educational opportunities over the past decade or so, and the lack of any real alternative to subsistence farming as a career. In the Upper Region, too, farming is a particularly unappealing life: the average holding is three acres, a unit that admits to the economic use of agriculture techniques no more advanced than the hoe.

In 1964 the White Fathers started their Agricultural Institute in Damongo. It has an 80-acre training farm, and its 30 students, all from up country, receive grants from the Government. The Government, too, pays its teachers, and as next year it has agreed to pay for some more, the institute will be able to double its annual intake of students. Buildings to accommodate them have been erected with grants from Oxfam and Misereor, the agency of the German Roman Catholic Bishops. There is no shortage of candidates to fill the new buildings. Schools in the Upper Region are regularly circularised about opportunities at the institute, and each mail-day brings about 15 applications to the mission at Damongo.

In Botswana we found that the problem of the ill-equipped school leaver went deeper than giving him an agricultural course of a couple of years. It is no different in northern Ghana. Here, too, a fairly advanced training is of little value unless the young farmer has the means to put his new skills into practice. To bring a boy from the Upper Region, turn him into a model farmer, and send him back to work on his father's three acres would be to do no service either to himself or his family. In most cases, indeed, his new-found sophistication would actually be resented at home. What must be provided is new land as well as new ideas. The White Fathers in Damongo found the solution in the land left by the Gonja Development Corporation. It appears, too, that they are doing considerably better than the organisers of the original scheme.

I met David Kumasi as he was walking to the fields for an afternoon's work. He is one of the 20 former students of the institute who have so far been settled on the land once occupied by the corporation. David has 15 acres, but these are added to the similar holdings of three of his colleagues, so that the four of them farm 60 acres as a co-operative. By their fathers' standards, this is a huge undertaking, but then David and his fellows are not farming it quite like their fathers.

Each co-operative of four has a small armoury of agricultural equipment including a tractor, a planter, a plough, and a corn-picker. The corn-pickers were provided by Oxfam which also funded some of the installations for the central compound in which the farmers live; the Czech cultivators they use were borrowed from the Government which has no shortage. Within four years, if profits remain as they are, the groups will be able to repay the loans on the larger items of equipment, and, as they invest in new machinery, so the old will devolve on their successors from the institute.

When David started work in the settlement a few years ago, he had no possessions other than the shirt and trousers in which he was dressed. So everything had to be on tick. The mission advanced him his fertiliser, his seeds, and all the diesel oil and maintenance costs for running the group's tractor. And at harvest time, the accounts would be settled. Naturally he was cautious at the beginning. But it has taken him only two years to appreciate the relationship between investment and profit. With a hefty application of fertiliser and the use of high-yielding maize, his group cropped 265 bags of grain from 35 acres last year. Worth just under £5 a bag, this made the group more than £1,000. Not all was profit by any means, but enough of it was to convince David that investment pays. He can now afford to be scornful of his juniors on the settlement who are as cautious as he once was, and almost speechless when asked how his father farms. 'These primitive methods . . .', he began, but the sentence ended incoherently.

David's progress from a background of subsistence farming to cash-cropping on this scale is an achievement that will benefit not just his own pocket. He has larger ambitions himself. 'I want,' he told me, 'to improve Ghana's agriculture and to improve my country.'

This is more than hot air. The north has a huge agricultural potential which is as yet quite untapped. Worse than that, the country imports a good half of its foodstuffs each year. And so ingrained is this reliance on assistance from outside that its people have conceived an unreasoning distaste for food raised by their own farmers. At the Agricultural Institute I visited a storeroom piled high with sacks of maize and of guinea corn produced by the young farmers on the settlement. Having previously seen so many grainstores packed with 'Bulgur' wheat – 'A gift from the people of the United States of America' stamped on each bag in half a dozen languages – this was one of the more refreshing sights of my tour. Yet

Brother Schrenk told me that it was difficult to sell because the local people were used to the imported varieties.

Brother Alex Schrenk comes from Germany, and runs the settlement and the Institute. He is not ordained, but like the fathers has sworn both to remain loyal to the society and to dedicate his life to Africa. In doing so, Brother Schrenk has put a formidable range of skills at the disposal of the continent. His family farms in the Black Forest, but he is more than a farmer. He is a qualified mason, a fine carpenter, and capable, too, of putting the most troublesome of his Porsche tractors (troublesome tractors tend to be given in aid) back on the road.

For Schrenk the aim of the farming school and the settlement is not simply to provide employment for school leavers. Nor does he find it difficult to justify the use of costly machinery. 'The fathers of these boys are just feeding their own families,' he says. 'They are not investing a penny in the land. With investment we can feed hundreds of people.'

There is certainly room for expansion on the land they have so far acquired from the Government. They received 1,000 acres, and only 300 have yet been cleared and cultivated. After that there are another couple of thousand acres once cleared for the groundnuts scheme. And as I stood with Schrenk on the side of a little river that marks the boundary of the old corporation's land, he pointed towards the thickets on the opposite bank. 'Over there,' he remarked, 'are a few thousand square miles with no one living in them. It is good agricultural country. We could build a road across this river one day.' David Kumasi has a more modest vision for the future: 'In ten years we will clear down to the river. Then we can farm 100 acres each.'

It would be to underestimate the White Fathers even to suggest that they might have left the hospital buildings idle for long. Soon after the corporation went bankrupt, they put an advertisement in our own *Catholic Herald* asking for nurses. It was answered by the Congregation of St Anne's, Wimbledon, which has 40 or 50 sisters in hospital and social work in the United Kingdom. Four of them arrived in Ghana in January 1955, and, with nine Ghanaian nurses, now run a hospital of 100 beds. I am no authority on how many nurses are required to staff a hospital of this size; I know only that year in and year out the sisters of St Anne's work double duties. They are very cheerful about it all, but they also appear very tired.

The West Gonja hospital covers an area too large to estimate; it is enough to say that 80 miles in one direction there is a Government hospital at Tamale, and 111 miles in the other there is one at Wa. As well as looking after their bed patients, the sisters and their junior staff deal with around 3,000 outpatients each month, and also run leprosy, maternity, and child welfare clinics both in Damongo and in the bush. Before May 1968, they travelled in an antique and fractious Opel estate car which had regularly to be pushed. Then Oxfam gave them a new Peugeot which helped a lot. *'Vainqueur au Safari '67'* says a notice stuck in the back window. That was a help, too.

It is not only medical hazards that the sisters have to cope with. The evening before my visit, a storm had lifted the roof of the children's ward from its walls, and deposited it in a clattering heap 15 yards away. No one was hurt. In Damongo, however, a number of women had been sheltering with their children against the mud wall of a local primary school. Its tin roof sloped, and so everyone had put their pots and pans under it to collect the water. At the height of the storm, one of the sodden school walls collapsed, crushing the water-gatherers beneath it, and killing a boy of 12 and a girl of eight. The dead and the injured were brought to the hospital where Dr Manuel Corachen, a Spaniard and its only doctor, patched up the wounds. He had also performed five operations that morning, but they were regular surgical cases and not at all an abnormal workload.

When Dr Corachen arrived in Ghana last year, he had elaborate plans for campaigns of preventive medicine. 'But I am one doctor to 100 beds,' he says. 'There are emergencies every day. I do only the curative.' Even that was not easily done at the beginning. The electricity supply for the hospital came from two wheezy and capricious generators; often one of them would fail, and occasionally both would black out together, leaving Corachen in his operating theatre with no more light than the glow of an oil lamp. Oxfam eased this situation by despatching a brand new generator to Damongo last year. Indeed, without such help from abroad the West

Gonja hospital could hardly continue as the efficient institution it is.

Government grants do not cover its costs, and the gap could never be filled by patients' fees; the equipment it receives from the Government amounts to what is left over when their own hospitals have stocked up. Such bodies as the United Nations or our Ministry of Overseas Development would not trouble themselves over one bush hospital in northern Ghana. So for decent equipment it relies on the charities. War on Want, for instance, has given enamel-ware and plasters, and its linen and blankets came from Holland. 'Without that gift,' said one of the sisters pertly, 'no linen, no blankets.'

If you want to see Dr Corachen at his most Latin, talk to him about the children. He will speak with knowledge and concern, of course, about other things like guinea worms and hook worms – of these he can show you some revolting photographs – and malaria and river blindness and tuberculosis. But it is the children who really anger him.

For the first five months of their lives, he says, they are well fed on their mother's milk – not perfectly fed, mind you, because mothers neglect any feeding rhythm by giving milk whenever they cry – but they are adequately fed all the same. After five months when they should be weaned on to a diet that will last until they can eat proper food, their mothers continue to feed them. By this time the milk is deficient in both protein and minerals, and so the child's health begins to deteriorate. Moreover it is fed like this for up to two years, and then expected to take straightaway to an adult diet. The result is that most of the children between seven months and three years around Damongo are malnourished. It is no coincidence that the word given to describe the pitiful condition of the acutely malnourished child is West African in origin: *kwashiorkor* means 'the sickness a child gets when another is born.'

What makes Corachen fume is that malnutrition can so easily be avoided. To prove the point, his wife Jacqueline has brought up their pretty baby daughter Saby in no less harsh conditions than those confronting a Ghanaian mother in the bush. At least, an electric light does not help much in rearing a child, and for Jacqueline the tinned and bottled baby foods of the West are unobtainable.

So regularly she visits the market in Damongo, and buys the green leaves of cassava plants which ordinarily go for nothing. Stallholders blink a bit, it is true, but she carries off bundles of these along with yams, which resemble our own potatoes, and eggs. These ingredients make an admirable baby food, brimming over with protein, but do local mothers use them? Jacqueline's cook who helps prepare Saby's food has a wife at home with an ailing child. Why not, she asked him, tell her to feed her baby as I feed Saby? 'No,' replied the cook, 'I dare not interfere with her running of the house; it is not my responsibility.'

Corachen and his wife have done their best to influence local mothers. The other day the doctor packed three of them off to his home to see how Jacqueline looked after Saby. And he has taken to refusing to see cases of malnourishment unless the mother arrives in his consulting room with bags of greenery and eggs. The misuse of eggs particularly enrages him. As we saw at the beginning of the chapter, they are kept to be given as presents until they rot in their shells. It is also the height of discourtesy to refuse them. But the usually well-mannered Corachen has not accepted an egg yet.

West Gonja hospital should have two doctors. Before Corachen arrived, it was without any for eight months. The sisters think him the best they have had, but his contract is limited, and by the time this book is read he will be in Barcelona. Ghana's new medical schools produce their first 30 doctors this year. Not many will be inclined to work in the bush, just as few promising graduates from training hospitals in London would want immediately to inure themselves in Tannochbrae: there are richer pickings in the world's capitals. But the sisters will still be in Damongo, and managing without a doctor is no novelty.

Several of the White Fathers in Tamale spoke during my stay of the ecumenical spirit that was now animating much of the missionary work in northern Ghana. To be honest, I saw no evidence of it on the ground. But by the same token I did not encounter any of the fruitless bickering between sects that still demeans Christian activity in some other parts of the world. It was, after all, Father Estaban who introduced me to John F. Dieterly, an American pastor in the United Church of Christ and currently field secretary for the Christian Service Committee in northern Ghana.

As well as running programmes of food distribution and of 'social advancement', a euphemism for clothing the naked, this Protestant organisation has five agricultural stations in the north. One of them is near Tamale at Mile 7, so called because it is that far from the town on the Damongo road. It is sited on one of Dr Nkrumah's 100 State farms, and shares a purpose with the White Fathers' Institute and settlement at Damongo. Atza van den Broek of the Dutch Reform Church, who runs it, was determined to show that a man setting out on a farming career could earn as much money as a teacher. Van den Broek was away when I visited Mile 7, but he is the sort of person about whom stories circulate. It is said that he was attending a prayer meeting in Holland when a churchman from Ghana stood up and cried: 'O Lord, send us an agriculturalist.' With a fine sense of biblical occasion, van den Broek replied: 'Here am I. Send me.'

There is no mechanisation at Mile 7 other than a small diesel pump which draws water from a leaky dam repaired by van den Broek when he started the project two years ago. As closely as possible their conditions resemble what the students will find after training. Athough they are taught the value of fertiliser and seed-selection, most of the food grown on their plots of two and a half acres is for consumption at home. It is in their keeping of sheep and of chicken that the students are expected to make a respectable living. 'Keeping sheep and poultry,' says Dieterly, 'is a very different matter from owning them. Farmers around here *own* their animals, and some time or other I see half of them in my front yard.'

The ten trainees who have so far joined van den Broek at Mile 7 are paid a labourer's wage of about £2 a week. From this they are obliged to save 5s. so that they will afterwards have money for small investments on their new farms. During training, too, they receive loans to buy fertiliser, seed, poultry, and chicken-feed. This is where Oxfam comes in. Such is the seasonal fluctuation in the price of maize that no small farmer can afford to feed poultry throughout the year. So Oxfam has provided the capital to buy a store of it at harvest time for general distribution in the area at a fixed price of £2.10s. a bag. The only person who fails to benefit from this is the local speculator who can buy maize at £2 a bag after the harvest and sell it at two or three times the price at the end of the season.

In the last few months three trainees have been settled on fresh land at Mile 3. The clever reader will note that its name is similar to that of Mile 7. The difference is that Mile 3 is on the Kumasi road. Driving up to it, the ignorant visitor would be quite unaware that either thought or money had gone into the settlement. This in itself is a good sign: at the beginning of his career, the cash farmer need look no different from the farmer who grows crops just to keep his family alive.

Salifu, a man somewhere in his thirties with an already large family, quickly disabused me of this first impression of Mile 3 by producing his accounts. They are kept in a well-thumbed notebook, and show quite clearly the advantages of van den Broek's scheme. During his two years of training, Salifu saved £20; he also made a profit of £25 from raising 200 broiler chickens for the local market. All this has been consumed by the cost of setting himself up in business – a chicken house (£14), roof tiles (£2.10s.), 50 chicken (£40), and a bag of feed (£2.10s.). But Salifu is already selling fresh eggs at 8s. a dozen, and has a current balance of £6.

Impressed by this achievement, I next asked Salifu about his crops. He told me he was growing yams and rice. The rice he would try and sell, and the yams he would 'chop', pidgin English for 'eat'. Was he using fertiliser on his rice? No, he wasn't. John Dieterly winced perceptibly. Was he then planting the seed in rows? No, he was broadcasting it. Dieterly chewed hard on the stem of his pipe. You cannot win every battle in the development war.

8 Escape and Refuge

'And when they say, "My whole body hurts", it's malaria.'

Gillian Streeter, volunteer nurse in Senegal

Students of comparative ideology should have two books about Portuguese Guinea on their shelves. The first, entitled *The Liberation of Guiné*, is by Basil Davidson, one of Africa's better-known historians. Dedicated in part 'to the memory of those who have died for the revolution of our times', it describes the progress of a well-armed revolt against the Portuguese in this, their tiny West African territory. At the back of the book Mr Davidson inserts a map to show how two-thirds of the country are now 'liberated', how some regions are 'contested' and how others, as well as many of the large towns, are still held by the Portuguese.

The second, a more modest affair, is written by John Biggs-Davison, Conservative MP for Chigwell, and is published by a London public relations firm. Called *Portuguese Guinea – Nailing a Lie*, it suggests that Basil Davidson has exaggerated the success of the rebellion, and that we in Great Britain have a duty to support Portugal in her war because she 'takes more seriously than some of her allies the Communist design of enveloping Europe from Africa'.

What makes Mr Biggs-Davison and his fellow travellers particularly nervous is that the nationalists have ambitions in the Cape Verde islands, about 500 miles off the coast and also owned by Portugal. Indeed, some of the leaders of the rebellion came from these islands. Should they fall into revolutionary hands, runs the argument, our sea route round the Cape will be in danger. It will be recalled that before aeroplanes were invented and in the days when ships had to dock regularly to take on coal, this was our only way to the Empire.

These brave books have one thing in common : they pay

only the scantest attention to the civilian casualties of the war. In fact, I cannot recall having seen the word 'refugee' in either of them. This is a failing that is generally common both to the tacticians of insurgency and to the strategists of repressions.

Africans began crossing the northern border of Portuguese Guinea* into Senegal early in 1964. By April there were 6,000 of them, two months later there were 20,000, and by July there were 25,000. In February 1965, it was reported that there were at least 45,000 and in June 1967 there were 60,000. The latest and most accurate figure is 68,400.

Some 4,000 have settled over the years in Dakar, the capital of Senegal and formerly of French West Africa. Like other big cities, Dakar had long exerted a pull on rural labour and the refugees from Portuguese Guinea came looking for work. Many, however, have been disappointed, and some have resorted to petty crime to make a living.

The other 64,000 tribesmen, more firmly rooted in the agricultural life they had left, travelled no further than the province of Casamence in southern Senegal. Not the least of the ironies here is that Casamence was Portuguese until 1886. It was then ceded to France in exchange for territory in the Congo.

Wedged between Portuguese Guinea to the south and that curious flowering of British Commonwealth culture, the Gambia, to the north, Casamence is what one imagines equatorial Africa to be. Much of it is deep forest, but elsewhere thick vegetation gives way to clearings for banana groves, for pasture, for fields of millet, and for groups of neatly-ordered grass huts. Along the great Casamence River, paddy vies with water lily for possession of its sodden banks, and everywhere there are trees – the huge, mis-shapen baobab, four or five varieties of palm, and flames of the forest, what the French call *flamboyants*.

In normal times Casamence supports a population of about 600,000. An additional 60,000, however thickly spread, would have been burdensome enough. But the majority of the refugees fled to areas already inhabited by their tribal kinsmen. Thus just two departments in the province, Kolda and Sedhiou,

* *Pace* Mr Davidson, I shall use the 'unliberated' name throughout. Portuguese Guinea is not yet independent.

have received 48,000 immigrants in the last six years. Their numbers, their lack of any means to earn a living at the beginning, and in some cases their political sympathies, have imposed numerous problems on the administrators of the province. It is no accident, for instance, that the governor of Casamence and the prefects of all its departments are army officers. The Portuguese conduct regular raids over the border to entice peasants back to their homes – sometimes by the most unsubtle of methods – and have recently taken to bombing villages suspected of harbouring nationalists.

The Senegalese authorities can themselves deal with the security problem. But in providing for and resettling the refugees, they have relied from the beginning on help from outside. Oxfam received its first news of the deteriorating situation in Casamence during the summer of 1964. What was urgently required were tools for cultivation and medicines to prevent epidemics of yellow fever, smallpox, and malaria. In September an emergency grant of £5,000 was sanctioned for these purposes, and 5,000 blankets and 100 tents were also despatched. It was soon clear, however, that the strain of a swelling population could not be relieved by private agencies alone. So Senegal applied to the United Nations for help, and an office of the United Nations High Commissioner for Refugees (UNHCR) was established in Dakar in 1965.

Run at present by Mr Mohamed Benamar, a highly efficient and sympathetic Algerian, the UNHCR in Senegal will have spent more than £400,000 on the refugees in five years. Its financial assistance is due to end next year, after which the office will deal with issues such as the legal status and the occasional repatriation of refugees. On top of this £400,000, private agencies and interested governments (usually those least interested in an alliance with the Portuguese) have contributed around £3 million towards resettlement and welfare works. Oxfam, for example, followed its emergency grant of £5,000 with a gift of £20,000, some of it from Oxfam of Canada, to help the UNHCR carry out its programme. In part it was relief work: the transport of food, the cost of mobile health teams, and the construction of clinics in the bush. The rest was spent on digging walls, veterinary services, land clearance, and the provision of more agricultural tools. Oxfam has maintained its interest in the mobile medical teams; last year it bought drugs and other supplies worth £850, and sent them to Senegal.

From the town of Kolda, Gillian Streeter conducts four medical safaris a week. She is one in a line of British nurses who have manned mobile clinics in the department since the emergency began.

After qualifying as an SRN in Canterbury, Gillian trained for a year in midwifery at Portsmouth, and for three months practised as a district midwife there. Her eye, however, was on more distant horizons. Having read *Two Ears of Corn*, an earlier account of Oxfam's work, and a book on the British volunteer agencies, she applied to the United Nations Association, and was told she would be going to Senegal. Gillian admits that she had never heard of the place, but had by chance read of Singalese soldiers, and so looked for Kolda on a map of Ceylon. Tracing the country eventually to West Africa, she spent three weeks brushing up her French, a few days acquainting herself with tropical medicine, and then set off. There are now few people with a more intimate knowledge of the department of Kolda.

The UNA should have two nurses in Kolda. As it is, Gillian is there alone, and making equally light of frequent break-ins at her house and news of fresh Portuguese bombing. In theory, too, there should be Senegalese nurses in the bush capable of bringing medical attention to its inhabitants. But they are under-trained, and are given only mobilettes to do their rounds; five of them cover a department of 220 square miles. Kolda itself, a town of 20,000, is badly enough served. Despite its two trained Senegalese nurses and a midwife who run clinics for young children, expectant mothers and lepers, the hospital there has had no doctor for some months. Instead it is visited once a fortnight by a doctor from Velingara, 60 miles to the east. True, there is a splendid dentist's at Kolda; but it has no electricity and no dentist. So one of the nurses does all the tooth extractions.

To bring effective medical attention to the bush around Kolda, Gillian reckons that each area should be visited once a week. When there were two very mobile nurses working in the department, this was just possible. Gillian would take the area, say, to the west of Kolda, and Penny Jones, who was repatriated some months ago after catching hepatitis, would take the east. Together they could hold eight clinics a week. Now Gillian does it all, and can visit most areas only once a fortnight. Moreover, the prefect of Sedhiou has begged her to hold clinics in his department and so she has taken on an additional 14 villages. These she can visit no more than once in six months. Like much of her normal work, she describes it as useful and rewarding in the short term, but of less value in the long term. And, she adds, there are some areas even in Kolda department which she simply cannot cover.

Gillian's safaris are conducted by well-equipped landrover. She has a driver, who is well enough paid by the Senegalese Red Cross to have invested recently in another wife, and two medical aides. They act as dressers, and translate her French into the local dialects. Neither of them has been properly trained for the job: one had just happened to work in a hospital in Dakar for a few months, and the other used to be a monkey-catcher.

Mobile though this outfit certainly is, it would be misleading to suggest that it brings medical attention direct to the people's huts. Sara Teneng, for instance, the village that Gillian visited one Monday morning during my stay in Kolda, has been told of the team's arrival the week before. Word had filtered through the bush, and some patients had walked distances of six, seven, and eight miles to attend the clinic; the frontier with Portuguese Guinea is just five miles away.

We started rather late from Kolda that morning, and it was not until 9.15 that Gillian set up shop under a spreading mango tree in Sara Teneng. I did not keep count of the number of patients she treated. Indeed, to have done so would have been a considerable task. For each time I turned my back on the clinic to look at the village or its surroundings, she had treated another. Gillian had not kept very close track either. Her estimate at 12.15 was 100. By the standard of some of her clinics, this was a modest figure. Her record is 350. But as she remarked to me in mid-consultation: 'An English GP would tear his hair out if he saw as many as this.'

As in surgeries all over the world, not all those who arrived in Sara Teneng during the morning were really sick. One or two farmers had sloped off work to complain of backache, and vastly enjoyed being massaged with pungent linament by Gillian's aides. A village elder sidled up to her at the end with a phial of penicillin which he had bought on the black market in Kolda, and asked if she would do the injection for him. What precise purpose it would serve he was not sure, but it would undoubtedly do him a power of good. Gillian staged a splendid fit of temper through an interpreter (not the easiest thing to do), confiscated the penicillin and threatened next time to tell the gendarmes.

'And how on earth,' said Gillian of another patient, 'do you *tell* if someone has a headache?' Yet among the 100 people she treated, a 'fair percentage', as she put it, was really ill. 'The children,' she said, 'they're always sick. About six out of ten die before they are four.'

Some of the children who came to the clinic at Sara Teneng were suffering from malaria which is endemic in Casamence. Gillian could reduce their fevers by administering pills sweetened with a spoonful of syrup, and hand their mothers more pills to ward off future attacks. But this, she said, was an unsatisfactory remedy, as Sara Teneng would not be revisited for some months. Other children had painful eye infections, the first signs of trachoma which can blind the sufferer. Some, too, had hook worms, parasites that bury themselves in the sole of the foot, work their way up through the body, and fall into the lung. Medicine to treat them is expensive, and Gillian is firm in its admistration. She tells mothers that she will not help their children unless they promise to buy them pairs of plastic sandals. The mothers always say they will, but Gillian is not confident that the inducement works.

Above all, of course, hovers the spectre of malnutrition. Its effect is a general deterioration of the child's health which lays him open to every disease that is found in Casamence. And its causes are the same as those we encountered in Ghana. Children are weaned at three years straight on to rice water which looks like milk, but possesses none of its other properties.

Eggs and greens and grain meal are all good for growing children, but here they have little of them. First the husband and bread-winner gets the first pick of the family's food – accounting in turn perhaps for the triviality of the complaints brought by men to Gillian Streeter's clinic – and his wife and children have the left-overs. There is also a taboo against eggs. If expectant mothers eat them, runs the local belief, they will produce weaklings, and if youngsters eat them, they will go blind. 'Both I and the other nurse,' says Gillian, 'wear glasses. I'm afraid that only confirms their superstitions.'

The team's landrover is large enough to take the seriously ill back to Kolda. There Gillian conducts afternoon surgeries in a storeroom at the hospital, and the chronically sick can go straight to bed. By the end of the morning a small queue had formed behind the vehicle. One of the patients was a pretty girl with a deep tropical ulcer in her foot; unless properly cleaned and regularly dressed, it would spread into a huge and suppurating sore. Another was an older woman suffering from gonorrhoeal arthritis.

We should, in fact, have taken far more patients than this back to Kolda, but some were plainly terrified at the prospect of a hospital and others complained that they could not leave their homes. One child, for instance, had been severely burnt on his hand and lower arm. The burn had become infected, and the infection had spread to his blood stream; his neck, his forehead and his groin were disfigured by revolting abscesses. Gillian told me that these would have to be incised in Kolda, and that his mother would have to spend ten days with him in the town: 'She is bound to have relatives in Kolda, and there would be someone to look after the house here. But she won't go. She says that her husband is away, and that she doesn't want to close the house down.'

Sara Teneng has about 100 residents. Of these only one family is from Portuguese Guinea. Baglo Diallo is a farmer, and came to the village with his wife and five children in 1965. He says that the nationalists advised him to leave, apparently for his own safety and not for theirs. He was lucky. Like most of the other tribesmen who have crossed the border, he had friends and relations on the other side. Diallo was also welcomed in Sara Teneng, partly perhaps because he was able to bring his own tools with him, and needed only some land to make a living.

Among the patients that Gillian treated that morning, there may have been many more refugees. It is difficult to tell as only one thing gives them away. The local people sometimes refer to her as '*Madame*', and if formally addressed by a refugee she would be '*Senhora*'. Certainly she never bothers to inquire where her patients are from: to do so, she says, would be to suggest that she is interested only in the locals. All in all, though, she reckons that one in five of her patients is a refugee. This, I suppose, would not satisfy the purist. But he should be thankful that the great majority of the 48,000 refugees in Kolda and Sedhiou are now assimilated among the local population. What is required and what Gillian is trying to provide is a little of the medical attention that her former patients in Portsmouth took for granted. When the UNA finally withdraws its volunteer nurses, it is hoped that the Senegalese Red Cross will find the personnel to take over the mobile clinics, and perhaps extend the principle throughout Casamence.

It is the refugees who have not been naturally integrated into their new surroundings that cause the problems. And the job of creating artificial settlements for them falls on Mohamed Benamar of the UNHCR in his capacity as adviser to the Senegal Government. For a start there are 5,600 Balante tribesmen from Portuguese Guinea who have lived since they arrived in Senegal as cattle thieves. They are to be given land near Bignona, north of the Casamence River, a solution that does not much please the local prefect.

Then there are the 4,000 refugees who arrived in Dakar. During my stay in Senegal I had long chats with two of them. The first was Dominic Mendy who until 1967 farmed in the village of Poulound, near Sara Pinto, in Portuguese Guinea. He left Poulound, he told me, because he was not interested in the war: he wanted neither to fight for the nationalists nor to be conscripted by the Portuguese. For it is one of Portugal's more dubious boasts that blacks fight cheerfully alongside whites to preserve her empire in Africa. Dominic had even less interest in 'volunteering' for service in Portugal's other two wars in Angola and Mozambique.

So he set out on foot with his family and two friends, and walked for three days to reach the coast. There they hitched a lift to Dakar by boat, and for three years Dominic worked as a labourer and house decorator whenever he was given a job.

The second was Pierre Mendy, unmarried and no relative of Dominic. He used to live in a village near Calicise which he computes as being three villages from the Senegalese frontier. For some years he had considered emigrating to Dakar to work, and in 1966 the Portuguese made up his mind for him. Their army, he told me, had come to the area looking for conscripts, and had commandeered animals and other farm produce. Pierre thought it time to leave. He travelled north to Bathurst, capital of the Gambia, and took a boat to Dakar. He worked there on and off for four years as a tailor in the handicrafts business.

For Pierre, Dominic and many others like them, the UNHCR has found an imaginative answer to their rootless existence in Dakar. When I met Dominic, he was being trained as a fisherman with 30 fellow refugees at Goudomp, a town on the Casamance River. After training, they will fish for the *cobbo*, a bony little creature which crowds these waters and is eaten in great quantities all over Senegal. Their supervisor thinks that they will make £18 a month out of the trade, a considerable sum by Senegalese standards. wenty miles down the road at Fanda, Pierre was building a house in preparation for his own resettlement and training. Building materials are being paid for by the UNHCR, and the Governments of Norway and Denmark have given £7,500 to cover the costs of fishing tackle, canoes, and little outboard motors.

The present plan is to settle 100 families from Dakar in fishing communities on the Casamance River. This will not empty the city of its refugees, but it will provide employment for those who are most in need. With the Balante rustlers out of harm's way, and with other tribesmen able to make a tolerable living from the land, it is possible to say that one chapter in refugee history is closed. Indeed, if it was not, the UNHCR would not be ending its resettlement and welfare work in Senegal. The situation next door in Portuguese Guinea, however, remains volatile, and another influx into Senegal waits on the turn of events there, not on the wishes of the United Nations.

I looked at the efforts of Oxfam and others to help refugees from Portuguese Guinea not because the organisation's commitment to them is thought to have been particularly effective. On this score, in fact, the projects have in the past rated a consistently dismal evaluation from Oxfam's staff at home and in the field. The big complaint was that there was a lack of co-ordination at the top. After a visit to Senegal, John Shiels, formerly Oxfam's Field Secretary for West Africa and now in India, wrote to his Field Director: 'I am *still* not sure whose project it is. . . .' Hethen listed off the organisations that were involved: International Voluntary Service, UNHCR, the Senegalese Red Cross, the UNA, the Government of Senegal, the prefecture of Kolda, the British Embassy, and the Senegalese Commission for Refugees. Of Penny Jones, the nurse who was then working from Kolda, he wrote: 'Never has a hard-working nurse slaved away so hard in the bush while so many high-powered pundits chased each other around the capital city in ever decreasing circles, each claiming to direct in some way the activities out in the bush.'

The reason for my own visit was that Senegal just happened to be on my route. In truth, it would be a remarkably pre-scribed tour of the developing world that avoided its refugees. In Africa alone, the UNHCR has almost one million on its books. There are negroes from the Southern Sudan, Moslems from Ethiopia, 67,000 Congolese, 160,000 Rwandese, and so on in miserable progression. The war in Nigeria set around 6 million people on the dreadful tramp for survival. Unless religious intolerance subsides, unless the architects and would-be architects of Africa's nation states put humanity before politics, the number of displaced people will doubtless continue to grow. Meanwhile charities and sympathetic governments will, I suppose, continue to provide as much as their funds can buy.

Some of Oxfam's contributions over the decade serve only as an illustration of this response: £35,000 for Sudanese refugees in Uganda, over £300,000 for Rwandese refugees in four countries bordering on Rwanda, £200,000 for Congolese casualties in the first months of the civil war, and £462,000 to Nigeria in the two years of her own civil war.

Other emergencies come to mind elsewhere in the world. The Palestinian refugees, uprooted from their homes by the establishment and subsequent expansion of Israel, now number 1½ million. In one grant among several to Palestinians, Oxfam gave £150,000 after the war of June 1967 to enable those in the camps to be properly fed. In the aftermath of the Jordanian civil war in September 1970, the organisation sent £15,000 as well as blankets and clothing through the Red Cross. The war in Vietnam has made more than a million people homeless, many of them dependent on relief supplies. Oxfam is active there, and has, unlike some agencies and governments, made grants to the North. The Chinese invasion of Tibet in 1959 and

1960 threw 60,000 refugees on to international charity in Nepal and India. Over the decade Oxfam has made more than 50 grants for their resettlement and welfare, ranging in value from £96. 15s. to £10,000.

Their needs are much the same as those of the refugees in Senegal. They have first to be kept alive, and then given the means to make a living. Money spent on them is not always an investment for the future; nor is there often the exciting return on capital that Oxfam can claim for its development projects. Those that are reached in time, however, do not starve, and that is something.

9 With Jackson through Niger

'We need a morgue, too. When are you coming
again?'

Missionary doctor in Niger

Bill Jackson, Oxfam's Field Director for West Africa, did
60,000 miles last year. Half of them were by air, and half by
landrover. The 30,000 landrover miles he shared with his Togo-
lese driver, Théophile. Naturally Théophile had the larger
helping, but Jackson did enough of them to complain of a
mysterious affliction. He calls it 'landrover neck' and says that
it comes from craning forward in the driving seat to watch for
pot-holes in the road.

I first met Bill Jackson in Accra, the capital of Ghana,
which is some 120 miles along the coast from his base in
Lomé, the capital of Togo. While I flew north to meet the
White Fathers, he drove east to do a week's work in the office.
On the Friday evening, when more prudent people were looking forward to a comfortable weekend, we met up again at the
airport in Abidjan, capital of the Ivory Coast. Our next stop
was Ouagadougou, capital of Upper Volta. Here we were only
in transit, but Jackson braved the protests of an Upper Voltan
gendarme to pass some Oxfam letters to a French volunteer
who just happened to be hanging about at the airport. 'Better
than the postal service,' Bill said as we reboarded the aircraft.
Our destination was Niamey, capital of Niger which was due
for a routine six-monthly visit from the '*délégué regional de
l'Oxfam*'.

The Grand Hotel in Niamey has an excellent view of the
River Niger, a swathe of blue water illuminated by a cloudless
sky, and flowing between dazzling, sandy banks. I had little
time to enjoy it. After breakfast at seven, we were out in the
yard inspecting the landrover which Théophile had driven
from Lomé. He had been forced off the road by a truck on

the way up, had hit a rock and had ripped open a tyre. Drastic surgery, involving steel thread and a bodkin, had patched it up, and Jackson decided to risk it.

Niamey lies in the south western corner of Niger. To see the rest of the country, you must head east. For a gentle 90 miles, the road is tarred. Then for another 600 miles it is a dirt-track through the bush. After that there is no road at all. I soon appreciated why Jackson suffers from 'landrover neck'. The dirt roads of Niger have earned themselves the French word *escaliers* which we would translate in the context as 'washboards'. There are well-worn ruts every two feet or so for 600 miles. At moderate speeds they can jolt a vehicle and its occupants to dismemberment. To counteract this one travels at a steady 50 mph, flying from the top of one rut to another. This method has one drawback. It reduces the chance of ever seeing a really big hole. And to hit one at speed means a broken spring. Hence 'landrover neck'.

Other means of travel entail mild hazards, too. Among its internal routes, Air Niger flies a few times a week from Niamey to Maradi, in the middle of the country, and on to Zinder, in the east. The return flight is at night. Whether or not it keeps to schedule depends on where the pilot eats his dinner. If he takes it at Zinder, then the aircraft will reach Maradi on time, and depart on time for Niamey. Should he not have dined in Zinder, he may leave his plane at the aerodrome in Maradi, and go into the town for a meal – a lengthy process as the pilot is French. The flight may therefore be delayed a couple of hours. There is a third possibility. The pilot may not feel like eating at all en route, and so be in a hurry to reach Niamey. If this is the case, he will take off early from Zinder, and remain an hour or so ahead of schedule right through to Niamey.

A national airline and country roads, however inadequate, are just the trappings of a modern state. Niger's needs are far simpler, and yet far more formidable. Most of her people live in the dusty savannah of the south, bordering on Nigeria. As the vegetation thins out to the north, so too does the population. And in the far north of the country, bordering here on Mali, Algeria, Libya, and Chad, there is little but the desert, the nomads it supports, and the crazy Europeans who cross it.

No one who has read the book this far should be surprised by what Oxfam is asked for in Niger. Her people urgently need water both for their animals and for themselves, and medicine. Two men I met in Niger demonstrated the urgency of the case well enough.

Robert Schneider was an American Peace Corps volunteer who had just done two years in the country. He came to promote co-operatives, but became more interested in water. A big man with a practical turn of mind, he evolved a technique for drilling small-bore wells in dried-up river beds. Pipes are sunk to a maximum of 60 feet; generally, he says, water is found nearer the surface. He got his drilling equipment and the pipes through American aid, and drew up an elaborate programme to take in the driest villages around Dogondoutchi, a town some 170 miles east of Niamey.

The plan was that men from the villages on his route should transport all his material and equipment in an orderly progress from site to site. It did not work. Villagers from miles away would stand over him as he finished work at one well, grab all the stuff, and hike it enormous distances to their own waterless communities. This was no adventure in Niger's crushing heat; the villagers were simply desperate for water. Schneider gave up his plan, and followed his equipment.

The second person was the assistant prefect of Dosso, a town at the other end of the tarmac from Niamey. He was a portly and affable figure, dressed in a voluminous and beautifully embroidered jelaba. For a civil servant, he was also a man of engaging and outspoken views. He was scornful, for instance, of 'these coast Africans' who wilted under the heat of the interior, and owned to an admiration for his country's former French colonisers. His own house, he told us, was once occupied by the local District Commissioner. It has electricity, but the supply is erratic and his fan regularly breaks down in the hottest part of the afternoon. 'I sometimes lie there on my back,' he said, 'and wonder how on earth that poor Frenchman managed it.'

Turning the conversation to medical facilities in the country, I asked him roughly how many Nigerien doctors there were. He lifted one hand in front of him, and began to count them off on his fingers. Well, he said, there is so-and-so working in Niamey, and that other character in Niamey along with him, and then we have Dr Sekou here in Dosso, and the Minister of Education, he's a doctor, and the President's secretary, he's a pharmacist. How many in all, I asked, a little embarrassed at having such a situation revealed so laboriously. The assistant prefect's finger-count reached eight, and he emphasised that not all of them were practising. The official figure for Nigerien doctors working in the country is five. They serve a population of 3½ million. When one of them leaves his post, say, to attend a medical conference in Abidjan or Dakar, there are 20 per cent fewer. And some people doubt whether developing countries need help.

Water and medical facilities, these then are the critical deficiencies in Niger. With one exception – and that was to provide a tractor and equipment for a demonstration farm near Niamey – Oxfam's grants to date have been for these purposes alone. The organisation has not been very generous to Niger because its funds are limited, and the £150,000 or so which is now channelled through Bill Jackson each year has to cover 14 countries in an area the size of Europe.

One particular grant of £11,000 to sink bore-holes and provide water for cattle in eastern Niger fell foul last year of Oxfam's own temporary shortage of capital. The delay was not disastrous, but it was an unpleasant reminder of the organisation's dependence on a regular income from the public. And if more is to be done by Oxfam in Niger, then Oxfam must collect more.

As Field Director, Bill Jackson is not allowed any prejudices. But he takes some pride in the fact that Oxfam is the only British voluntary aid organisation to have mounted a proper programme in Francophone West Africa. Excluding Nigeria, which has been out of his orbit for the duration of the war, nearly 80 per cent of that £150,000 now goes to these nine countries each year.

And he admits to a certain dry-eyed sympathy for Niger itself. 'I'm very pro this place,' he yelled over the racket of his straining landrover engine. 'It's received four body-blows in just two years. First the war over Biafra stopped its trade in live cattle with eastern Nigeria. Then Ghana expelled all her aliens last year, and 40,000 Nigeriens arrived here overnight. Next there was a drought a couple of years ago that destroyed a third of the national herd – up to 80 or 90 per cent in parts of the north. And if that wasn't enough, the devaluation of the franc dragged the local currency down with it without as much as a by-your-leave from the French Government.'

For these and for other reasons, already made clear by Robert Schneider and the assistant prefect of Dosso, Bill Jackson thinks that Niger should be Oxfam's top priority in West Africa. This is not just one man's whim. He must consider the competing claims of other countries, and assess the calibre of the people who will administer the grants. Besides, it is not Jackson who makes the decisions; it is Oxfam's Africa Committee at headquarters. Nevertheless he made this recommendation to the committee in his last annual report, and it was accepted. And so when we set out from Niamey that Saturday morning, Jackson knew very roughly what could be spent in Niger – £22,000 over the year, or about 15 per cent of the Oxfam's entire West African budget.

Our first call was on the hospital in Dosso. It was a harsh introduction to the country's medical problems. Lying on her side in the shade of one of its terraces was a girl of nine or ten. A limp arm covered the side of her face. Her father squatted next to her with a fan held motionless in one hand. Around the child's head buzzed an ugly swarm of flies which neither she nor her father did anything to repel. There was no point. She was dead. Dr Sekou explained that she had been brought in at 12.15, and had died while we were having lunch. It was probably meningitis, he said. I recalled then a news item that I had seen in the Ghanian papers – 'Meningitis epidemic hits western Niger'.

Dr Sekou, who is in charge here, has the unenviable distinction of being the only Nigerien doctor working outside Niamey. The department of Dosso has a population of about ½ million, and he shares a responsibility for its health with just one other doctor, a Pole called Wozniczko who runs a hospital 90 miles away. There are, of course, nurses in the department, but only four of them are properly qualified. The figure he gives is one qualified nurse per 200,000 people.

It is hardly surprising therefore that he treated the little girl's death so matter-of-factly. 'Personal medicine,' he said, 'is decades away. We have to go forward on a much broader front.' To help him the World Health Organisation (WHO) has established in Dosso a pilot project for rural health in Niger.

Like Oxfam and every other aid organisation, WHO has to operate on the stingiest of budgets. It cannot, for example, afford to give Dr Sekou an operating theatre; that would be far too luxurious. What it can do, with additional funds from any agency prepared to support the project, is to provide the crudest elements in a primary health programme. It plans first to supply two drinking fountains for the town of Dosso; at present its 5,000 inhabitants rely on – and often fight over – three open wells. Next it wants to build latrines in Dosso; there are none at the moment. Then there should be drains to prevent storm water collecting in stagnant pools in the town which give its residents bilharzia. Rubbish dumps are needed, too.

Hand in hand with this campaign to improve standards of hygiene in Dosso will go a programme of health education in the rural areas. For Dr Sekou, the priority here is mother and child care. And he wanted Jackson to recommend to Oxfam a grant of about £10,000 to pay for a properly equipped centre in Dosso, and a landrover to bring people in from the bush.

From his regular Government budget, Dr Sekou could afford nothing of the kind. Eighty per cent of it goes on salaries, leaving just enough to build a tiny dispensary every four years. And WHO was interested more in hygiene and an anti-tuberculosis drive. Jackson was doubtful about the project. Would it not be better, he suggested, to operate exclusively in the bush, rather than to concentrate new facilities in the town? Why not, he added, put up seven smaller buildings around Dosso? No, replied Dr Sekou, we haven't the staff to run them. Besides, we need a new building at the hospital so that we can keep healthy mothers and children away from the sick. What about mobile teams, Jackson persisted? 'Our work must start,' said Dr Sekou, 'where we have the personnel.'

Bill Jackson was still unhappy about the scheme. 'I would certainly not recommend that we pay for any of their equipment,' he told me. 'They can get that at any time from UNICEF [the United Nation Children's Fund].' He knew, too, that he would be asked in Niamey for help in providing refresher courses for nurses in the same area. 'Perhaps Oxfam should concentrate on retraining these people,' he said. 'As a Field Director you can really go around in circles on this sort of thing.'

We pulled out of Dosso as the afternoon heat was rising to its shimmering peak. Our destination that night was the hospital run by the Sudan Interior Mission at Galmi, 200 miles to the east. We arrived well after nightfall, ate a good meal, washed the sand out of our hair, and went to bed. In all we spent 18 hours there. It was long enough just to scratch the surface of the place. Having scratched, I realise that only clichés do full justice to Galmi. It is in the middle of nowhere, it is an oasis in more senses than one, and it is in its way a wonder of the world.

When the Sudan Interior Mission wanted to build a hospital in Niger after the war, they approached the then French colonial administration for a site. The French were uneasy. First, virtually the whole population of Niger is Moslem; secondly, the SIM is composed of Protestant evangelicals; and thirdly, the French administrators were Roman Catholic almost to a man. And so they turned down the sites which the SIM proposed. Some were delightful locations on the banks of the Niger.

Being persistent people by nature, however, the SIM went back to the Government, and said they would build their hospital on any site they were offered. An exasperated Government gave them a plot of stony, windswept land outside an insignificant hamlet on the main road east.

Dr Burt Long and his wife have brought up five children at Galmi. Dr Long has also contrived to make a national legend out of a hospital. When a Nigerien tells you something is 'Galmi', he means that it is so utterly decrepit that only Galmi hospital could restore it. Long himself says that he has seen some miracles in his time, but that they are not the general rule: 'Our patients go first to the witchdoctor, then to the barber, then to the Moslem headman, and then they crawl in here to die.'

I confess I find it a little difficult to understand Dr Long. That an American surgeon should give up his career to work in the Nigerien bush for life is one thing. That he should sacrifice a huge income for a mission salary of £350 per year (with £17. 10s. deducted for the mission's 'building maintenance fund') is another. Dr Long, of course, is deeply religious, and Galmi hospital serves a religious purpose. I was there on a Sunday morning. There were three readings at breakfast – one from the authorised version of the Bible, another from a modern English translation, and a third of textual criticism. After breakfast, he conducted a Sunday school class in Hausa and preached at Matins in the hospital church. I watched as his congregation emerged from the service, the adults clothed, and most of the children naked. There were no more than a dozen adults, the sum total of Dr Long's evangelising work over 20 years. Yet even this does not dispirit him. And he continues to devote his skills to every sick person who arrives at Galmi.

He cannot run his hospital quite as he would run one in the States. For a start, there is the business of mattresses. So rapidly would they become fouled and infested that he does without them. Lengths of rush matting cover bare springs instead. The beds themselves and the space they occupy are in short supply. So a very real distinction is made between bed-patients and up-patients: the former have beds, and the others have the floor. There are 181 beds at Galmi; when I visited the hospital there were more than 250 patients being treated.

In an American hospital, food is cooked for the patients, and their relatives can visit only at prescribed hours. Neither of these things happens at Galmi. Relations would arrive with patients in any event, and they may as well cook for them: that way the hospital saves both money and labour. Some time ago, admittedly, Dr Long built 40 or so one-room concrete sheds so that relatives did not have to live in the wards. But the scheme never worked out as planned. The sheds are now occupied by 80 patients suffering from pulmonary tuberculosis.

Before we looked at the TB wing, Dr Long warned us not to get too close to the patients. Chatting range is spitting range, and pulmonary TB is highly infectious. Bill Jackson did not need the advice: he had been kept awake the previous night by their coughing.

All these TB cases are long-termers – five months and upwards. They divide themselves into two categories: those who will recover and those who will not. Dr Long talked to one who lay listless on his back in the shade. His limbs were wasted, his toes and finger-tips were bulbous, and his knee caps protruded like hammers. Occasionally he coughed. 'All symptoms of TB,' Dr Long said. 'He will probably die.' Others appeared healthy and cheerful. They had come in time, and their disease had been checked. They were on the mend.

To reduce the chances of cross-infection, Dr Long would be happier if these patients in particular were not accompanied by their friends and relations. But he goes along with local custom, and acknowledges, too, that the hospital does a considerable service in merely removing them from their homes where they could infect whole families. Similarly, he would prefer not to see chickens running around his hospital, but recognises that they provide valuable protein for his TB patients. 'See that grain,' he said, pointing to a pile of yellow dust quite indistinguishable from the sand around it. 'Someone's lunch.'

In the hospital proper, Long took us on a tour of the wards. There was one large female ward, and one large male ward, each with about 30 beds, and a number of smaller ones. The corridors were also well-populated. I recall only the TB cases. They should be stressed. A WHO committee has described tuberculosis as 'the most important specific communicable disease in the world', and a British medical authority says that 'the world is experiencing an epidemic of tuberculosis.'

The TB patients in the hospital were less infectious than those outside. They were suffering from non-pulmonary or genito-urinary tuberculosis. Its ravages, however, were no less apparent in this form than in the other. Dr Long showed us cases where the disease had attacked the spinal cord, and produced visible cavities in the vertebrae. In one side-ward, we were greeted by the most dazzling smile from a teenage girl. She lay on her stomach, her curly hair tightly plaited in the local fashion. A blanket covered her up to the small of the back. She was thin, but no thinner than many of her more healthy compatriots. 'Before the harvest,' Dr Long had told me earlier, 'some of these people go three days without eating.'

Then the doctor removed the blanket. Her buttocks were consumed by two large ulcers. 'Look,' said Long, 'it's healed up to here.' But the flesh and muscle of her legs were wasted, and the disease had cut her spinal cord. She would never walk again. Dr Long then passed some disobliging comments on the girl's parents who had kept her at home in this condition. 'We'll discharge her soon enough,' he said, 'but she will remain so weak that she will catch something else and be dead by the time she is 30.'

Stepping outside the hospital again, Dr Long showed us where he planned to build a new maternity unit. This was the reason for Jackson's visit. At present Galmi has seven maternity beds for up to 30 confinements a month. In normal circumstances, this would be tolerable. But Long says that they have a high percentage of abnormal births, and that one in every two babies is born dead. Mothers therefore have to stay in bed longer than usual. A proper maternity unit would have its own washrooms: 'I don't much like our mothers bathing in the same place as we wash down the corpses.' It would also have a labour room and a delivery room; all the deliveries are at present conducted in the operating theatre. This is far from satisfactory as Dr Jim Ceton, Long's assistant, and the Swiss midwife at Galmi will tell you. There was an occasion recently when the two of them juggled spectacularly with a surgical case and two deliveries in the same small room.

The cost of the new unit worked out at £3,750. Its equipment would be another £1,000. Dr Long hoped that Oxfam could provide most of this, and that he could appeal to his church in America for the rest. It is Bill Jackson's practice on these tours to be businesslike and unsentimental. He made careful notes on the project, and agreed to send Galmi's application through to Oxfam with his recommendation.

Our next stop was at a leprosarium also run by the Sudan Interior Mission at Dandja, ten miles south of Maradi and 30 miles north of Niger's border with Nigeria. There is much evangelism here, too. Leprous children attending the centre's school have bible classes, devotional hours, and Sunday prayer meetings. Every adult patient arriving at the leprosarium is contacted by an evangelist who explains the way to salvation. And at a twice weekly medicine line where patients receive their pills, the SIM people hold a full-scale service. If this sort of thing went on in hospitals and doctors' surgeries in England, I would be the first to protest. If, on the other hand, I was a Nigerien leper and a Moslem, my resentment would be muted. The SIM runs the only leprosarium in Niger.

It began in 1956, and since then has had 1,300 patients. Last year they discharged 92 as cured, and when I visited in June there were 315 under treatment. Some were no-hopers. The disease, which is caused by a germ closely resembling that of tuberculosis, attacks the peripheral nerves. In an advanced stage, it results in a complete loss of feeling in the feet, the arms, the nose, and the eyelids. And it is this lack of sensitivity rather than the disease itself which leads to the dreadful disfigurement commonly associated with leprosy. At the SIM in Dandja, there were patients whose drooping and powerless eyelids had caused near-blindness, and many more who possessed only stumps for limbs. Without their sensing it, their arms and legs had become bruised or ulcerated, burnt in fires at home or chewed by rats.

For others, the disease can be checked and reversed. With judicious use of medicine and by constant and well-supervised exercise, sensitivity will return to clenched and scrawny fists. And for those truly on the mend, there is more than enough work at the leprosarium to keep them occupied.

David Schultz, the Canadian missionary in charge, now runs a farm as well as a hospital at Dandja. It serves a more than therapeutic purpose. He wants first to show his young male patients that with fertiliser and with heavier planting, they can farm more successfully than their healthy relations. And he has proved the point amply by bettering a local millet yield of six bags per acre to 16 bags in a few years. At present the farm is supplying the leprosarium with half its annual requirement in grain. Schultz looks forward to the day when it will produce the whole lot. Considering he has to feed 50 school-children who are too young to work, and a number of patients who are too ill to do so, it would be no small achievement.

Oxfam has helped the leprosarium since 1966 when a plague of insects destroyed the crops in the area, and £300 was needed to feed its patients. More recently the organisation has given grants to clear trees and scrub for new agricultural land, to provide materials for the knitting and needlework that some of the patients do, and to buy a landrover. This vehicle ferries men from the leprosarium to the farm, and takes its produce to market in Maradi. 'I don't know what we would have done without it,' says Schultz.

Bill Jackson's advice was needed on a particular problem. It seemed that part of the rehabilitation work was not going well. Despite handicaps that appeared to me almost insuperable, patients were making some lovely children's clothes and woven cloth. This was fine. Where the project fell down was that they were unable to sell them locally at competitive prices. Schultz wanted to know whether £100 of the original grant of £300 made for the purpose could be used on the farm. With it they could clear a little more land for their rice, beans, groundnuts, millet, and cotton. Jackson promised to put the case to Oxfam.

In contrast to a small adjustment involving £100, Bill Jackson next considered a project costing more than £10,000. This was no modest missionary enterprise; it sought to improve the water supply for a population of 100,000. This represents one in 35 of Niger's people.

Mayahi is one of the *arrondissements* in the department of Maradi. It has at the moment 92 wells spread among its 317 villages. That the local authority should have totted them up is roughly the equivalent of the Metropolitan Water Board counting the number of taps in London. But then water is a more precious commodity in the semi-desert of Niger than it is in Lambeth. The wells that do exist certainly have to be as formidable structures as our own reservoirs, obligingly fed by the 'surface' water of a heavy rainfall and full rivers. The average depth of a well in Mayahi arrondissement is 160 feet, and every drop it yields must be pulled that distance by the women or by oxen.

It would be nice to think that one day some bright scientist would invent a way of shortening this back-breaking circuit. Applicants for the job are invited to the Nigerien bush latish any afternoon. At the well-sides people have laid tree trunks over which their ropes run. Gouged in the wood are deep trenches which go deeper each time a woman winches her bucket to the top. And on any decent well, convoys of women, all dangling pots and pans from heavy yokes, converge each day like galleons in full rig.

'Decent' is too vague a word to be used by OFEDES, the Office des Eaux du Sous-Sol, which put its project to Jackson. OFEDES builds wells to a precise formula. They should be seven feet in diameter, and cemented the whole way down. No well, it says, is worth the name unless it can be properly maintained, and is deep enough to provide water throughout the year.

In Mayahi it wanted to build 30 wells, some in villages where there was no water at all, and others where the supply dried up in the dry season. Their construction was to be a thoroughly co-operative, indeed international, effort. Villagers would provide the labour for nothing; the Government would pay the salaries of ten professional well-diggers, and also enable OFEDES to undertake the maintenance of the wells; two American Peace Corps volunteers would supervise their construction; and Oxfam was being asked for a landrover and the material for building the wells.

Bill Jackson is in his element on a project like this. Each Oxfam Field Director, I found, has a style of his own. Some concentrate on the broader aspects of a project. Jackson's is painstakingly to extract every fact and figure that may be relevant, and to furnish headquarters with so much information that queries are answered well before they are raised.

In Mayahi, he wanted to know at what depth each well might encounter water; how much reinforcing rods from Nigeria cost these days; the local price of cement; whether Oxfam would avoid import duty on the landrover – 'a condition of our aid'; whether the Government would really pay for the running costs of the project and so on. A mere reporter remained unwontedly silent. After one such session lasting the whole of an afternoon, Jackson courteously apologised to the prefect of Maradi for asking such a catalogue of questions. 'Never mind,' the prefect replied. 'Everyone who helps us asks a lot of questions.'

OFEDES planned to build the wells in ten months flat. It wanted, moreover, to start work on them soon. A delay of a few months in sanctioning the grant would mean that it would have to wait until the following dry season, and a whole year would be wasted. Oxfam rightly prides itself on its adaptability, and so an exception was made to its usual procedure. Through his Field Secretary in Oxford, Bill Jackson had given the Africa Committee an outline of the scheme before he left Lomé. At its June meeting, the committee approved in principle of a grant of £10,000. Provided Jackson was satisfied with the detailed plans and could later communicate them in full to headquarters, then the money could go to work. In fact, when Jackson came to examine the project in the field, he found he was being asked for a little over £13,000. 'Oxfam should be exonerated from tax and duties,' he told me. 'So we should be able to reduce it to £10,000.'

When I left Bill to return to Niamey, he was half-way through his tour of Niger. He drove next to Zinder, 150 miles to the east of Maradi. There he had both to assess prospective projects and report on established ones. Then he, too, returned to Niamey to spend the weekend visiting officials of the Government and of the international agencies.

Our paths were to have divided finally at Maradi. But UTA, the French airline which was ferrying me about West Africa, decided otherwise. They said that my flight did not exist, and that I would have to stay in Niamey for another 48 hours. I was therefore waiting for Bill when he returned from Zinder.

He is a man with a considerable fluency in figures, the product perhaps of a classical education at Trinity College, Dublin, and five years in the Oxfam office at Oxford. During a conversation held in a hotel bedroom at 2 o'clock one morning, he gave me six notebook pages of them on his trip thus far.

Requests, he said, totalled £46,500. That was twice as much as Oxfam could at present afford in Niger: 'We could, however, sponsor some first-rate projects at £21,000.'

He was disinclined to support the mother and child centre at Dosso, and thought it better to help with the retraining of nurses. This would involve £1,750 for a landrover and the running costs of the programme. Next there was £100 for the leprosarium, and £10,000 for the wells at Mayahi.

Out east, he was asked for a grant for a cattle-watering project established by the UN Food and Agriculture Organisation and the United Nations Development Fund. Oxfam had already helped here, and now the project wanted a new pump station and a tractor to build fire-breaks. Bill explained that the Lister generators for the original scheme had only just arrived on site, and that 'Oxfam could not consider an additional grant until they are installed'.

Then there was equipment for a bush hospital and money for a seed co-operative both managed by a Roman Catholic mission way up North. The French father in charge had driven to Zinder to discuss the application with Bill. A func-

146

tional literacy campaign run by the Nigerien Government and by the Peace Corps near the town needed funds, and a former Peace Corps doctor wanted a water and electricity supply for his hospital.

The successful projects will eventually rate perhaps no more than one-line entries in Oxfam hand-outs. But each represents the work – sometimes for life – of men like Dr Burt Long. Bill said he would strongly recommend that Oxfam give Galmi a proper maternity unit.

10 Alternatives

'I sit on a man's back choking him and making him
carry me and yet assure myself and others that I
am sorry for him and wish to lighten his load by all
possible means – except by getting off his back.'

Leo Tolstoy

Changing planes at Madras airport, in southern India, I met a
Russian engineer. He told me he had been teaching for three
years in a technical college in West Bengal. In return, I told
him I was writing a book about the work of a private aid
organisation called Oxfam.

Was there a political side to this work, he asked? 'No,' I
replied. 'Oxfam receives no money from Government, and has
no political biases.' 'Where then does it get the money?' 'From
the public.' 'Tins?' he inquired, incredulous. 'Yes, there are a
lot of tins.' 'That's very good,' he said, 'but I think you have
misunderstood my question. Are the people who put their
money in the tins aware of the political side?' 'What political
side?' 'That British and other western companies are operating in India, exporting their profits and only a proportion of
these profits is coming back to India as aid.'

I was disinclined then and there to argue the toss with a
good Marxist on the merits or otherwise of private investment
in developing countries. That there are merits is certain. First,
the establishment of factories involves the transfer of techno-
logy from the more developed to the less developed parts of
the world. It also means that local managers and workers gain
skills and training that they would not otherwise possess;
new jobs are created, and the companies contribute to local
revenue through taxation; local business is often stimulated,
and overseas markets are opened up for them. If such advantages did not exist, governments of developing countries would
not currently be offering inducements to attract private in-

vestment from overseas. And there would be no UNIDO (United Nations Industrial Development Organisation) to sponsor it.

That there are drawbacks is equally apparent. The *New York Times* reported recently that in just one year the Latin American subsidiaries of companies in the United States had repatriated £425 million in profits. This figure represents more than double what the whole region received during the same period in new private investment and foreign aid put together.

Moreover, local subsidiaries often act more in the interests of their parent companies than in response to local needs. They introduce industries that employ only a few people (what economists call capital intensive rather than labour intensive industries), site them in areas where there is less unemployment than an abundance of raw materials, and pay their workers artificially high wages. And so powerful are foreign investors that in some cases they are able not only to interfere in the politics of developing countries, but actually to dominate them. Hence that old tag: 'What is good for the United Fruit Company is good for the United States.'

Private investment is just one aspect of the relationship between the rich world and the poor world. Another is trade. Everyone knows that British goods can be bought throughout the world, and that we are, give or take the odd dock strike, a great trading nation. Poor countries would like to emulate us.

In trying to do so, they have much in their favour. For as long as Europeans have known about a wider world they have been interested in its raw materials. In part, this interest once accounted for our colonising large chunks of it. And we have retained our interest. Senegal exports peanuts to Europe for processing as vegetable oil, margarine, soap, and animal feed; Ghana produces cocoa; Brazil produces coffee; the West Indies produce sugar; Zambia mines for copper; Venezuela drills for oil and so on. It sounds lovely.

The problem is this. Developing countries rely on primary products for almost all their overseas earnings. Half of them, in fact, are dependent on just one commodity for more than 50 per cent of their export receipts. They are therefore at the mercy of the international commodity agreements which exist – or more often do not exist – to control the market and its price. Ghana is a case in point. Cocoa produced in the fertile regions of her hinterland accounts for two-thirds of her exports. From 1953 to 1961 they increased by 71 per cent. But because of a fall in cocoa prices at the time, her revenue from these exports rose by only 23 per cent. And during the same period she faced an increase of 11 per cent in the price of the manufactured goods which she has to import.

There are two ways in which developing countries can avoid this depressing equation. Both have been rigorously canvassed at successive meetings of UNCTAD (the United Nations Conference on Trade and Development), but without many practical results. The first is that the rich countries should agree to further arrangements which will ensure a fair, stable, and gradually increasing price for the raw materials they buy from developing countries. Secondly, and more pertinently, they should enable the poor countries to process some of their raw materials themselves.

This second expedient could be fairly easily applied. The consequence of any relaxation in current tariff and quota restrictions by the developed countries would be to encourage industrialisation in the developing world. It would, however, entail a minor revolution in the relationship between the rich and the poor countries. For in the past American and European industry has looked upon countries outside not as rivals but as markets. And traditions die hard. How hard exactly can be judged by the pressure put on the Brazilians a few years back when they decided to manufacture their own instant coffee. The American manufacturers complained to their Government of 'unfair competition', the American Government protested to the Brazilian Government and the luckless Brazilian manufacturers now face a punitive export tax on instant coffee. It is a tale to be borne in mind when next watching the television advertisement that portrays cheerful Brazilians shaking Maxwell House coffee beans.

Cotton provides us with an eloquent example of how the whole process works. In its raw and cheapest state, cotton can be imported freely into this and into other developed countries. But should the producing country open a factory to make its cotton into cloth, it will no longer be able to export it so easily. Tariffs will see to that. And if the producing country is foolhardy enough to make its cloth into shirts, there will be even higher tariffs. Quotas, too, often ensure that a producing country, however efficient its shirt factories, cannot increase the sales to the developed world. Here, of course, it may be argued that the governments of developed countries have a duty to protect their own ailing textile industries. They also, as the developing countries point out, have a far less serious unemployment problem, a system of social security benefits, and splendid facilities for retraining workers in areas of industry that will remain competitive for decades.

In some areas tariff barriers are being eroded. But this is the result less of a nation's generosity to its fellows than of hard bargaining: 'if you allow us to enter your markets, we will let you enter ours.' The developing countries have little with which to bargain. They also depend on the more sophisticated markets of the West because their own neighbours are generally too poor to buy from them. So development economists argue that the principle of tariff reform should be extended to developing countries, whether or not it is to the immediate advantage of the developed. Some have gone further, and coined the phrase 'Trade, not aid.'

Aid is popularly regarded as huge cash hand-outs from the rich countries to the deserving, and sometimes not so deserving, poor. This view has to be reconciled with the facts.

Last year Britain applied a total of about £420 million in aid to developing countries. Just half of this went in private investment which was expected to make a profit for our countrymen. Of the rest, part took the form of loans from the British Government and part went in grants. Loans can play as valuable a role in financing development projects as gifts. But however 'soft' or 'long-term' their interest rates, they also have a nasty habit of being paid back – in full. Thus it is estimated that two-thirds of the aid sent to developing countries is repaid each year to the developed world, either in capital or in interest. And this proportion is increasing. At the present rate of aid expenditure, economists say, its entire benefit will soon be offset in this way. Brazil already finds herself in the anomalous position of paying back more than she receives.

There is another, more palpable, way in which countries like Britain benefit from the aid they send overseas. In 1968, the last year for which I have details, 58 per cent of British aid was 'tied', an expression meaning it was give on condition that it be spent on our own manufactures and services. This form of aid does wonders for the British balance of payments situation, but can have less desirable results for the recipients. They have to buy British goods where others may be cheaper, and start grandiose development projects where cheaper ones may be more effective.

Just as Britain gains formidable trading advantages from aid, so too can she use it as a diplomatic weapon. When Tanzania broke off relations with Britain over Rhodesia, our Government stopped payment on a loan of £7 million. And when, more recently, Tanzania decided not to pay the pensions of those colonial civil servants who had left the country after independence, Britain cancelled the rest of her aid programme.

Despite the ways in which Britain leavens her bounty, there remain those who are unhappy about our generosity. Reviewing Britain's financial position in May 1969, no less a figure than Sir Leslie O'Brien, Governor of the Bank of England, said: '. . . the second change for the worse has been the huge increase in Government expenditure abroad mainly on aid to less developed countries and for defence . . . This has been extremely worrying and I am glad at last the increase has been checked and is beginning to give place to a modest fall.' Sir Leslie's statement deserves examination.

It is interesting first that defence expenditure as well as aid should have risen steeply during the sixties, the period of which Sir Leslie was speaking. For Britain is currently spending more on defence than the whole of the rich world spends on aid. Secondly, it is nice to know that Sir Leslie approves of a 'modest fall' in our aid bill. For Britain has publicly committed herself to contributing each year 1 per cent of her gross national product to the developing countries. This proportion, which may include all private investment and all official assistance, has been met twice in the decade – once in 1961 and again in 1964. Since then, to use the Governor's word, it has been 'checked'.

Is it worth our ever fulfilling the promise? Some members of the aid lobby would say that we had a moral duty to do so. Morality, however, does not always play a conspicuous part in Government practice. Others would say that unless we increase our aid, such tension will arise between the rich and the poor countries that sooner or later there will be war. We, after all, invaded their land to help *our* industrial revolutions; they may do the same to help *theirs*. To take this view of things, however, requires a vision not always apparent in public life.

A stronger argument must be deployed. It is this. Britain is a trading nation, with traditional links through the Commonwealth with many developing countries. To help them develop further would enhance their capacity to buy British goods. Already we receive $12\frac{1}{2}$ per cent of the orders which are placed with the rich countries by the poor. And our aid to them accounts for only $6\frac{1}{2}$ per cent of the total contribution. This argument, of course, has a general application. Economists like Barbara Ward argue that the present lopsided relationship between rich and poor countries presents a threat to the continued prosperity of the rich.

The aid that Oxfam disburses is neglible compared with the sums that governments can command. Oxfam's aid is not even recorded in official British statistics. But it is as well not to dimiss the overall effect of the world's voluntary agencies. In 1968 they gave an estimated £240 million, far more than the British Government. Most came from the United States, and Britain contributed only a twentieth of the total. But no one would deny that, pound for pound, Britain's voluntary aid was more effective than that of any Government. Little of it was sent in the form of loans, it sought no profit, and it served no diplomatic purpose.

Oxfam, the largest of the British voluntary agencies, is in business neither to save its own conscience nor to please governments. Its aid is sent in response to local needs. These are readily discernible. But it is one thing to feel sorry for a beggar, for a starving farmer or for a leper, entirely another to bring some permanent improvement in his condition. In India I came across two cases in which philanthropy had been wondrously misapplied.

After the famine in Bihar, an organisation in Britain shipped out high-powered drilling rigs to sink new wells, and an ex-army mobile workshop to renovate old wells and pumpsets in the State. The drilling rigs were a godsend to the farmers who could afford the service, less useful to those who really needed help; the mobile workshop was so expensive to run that it has been abandoned by the roadside.

And as part of their contribution to the family planning project of the Christian Medical Association of India, the Swedish Baptists sent to Bangalore 2½ million male contraceptives. As sheaths go, they were very classy. Called 'Million Gold' and made in Japan, they would have cost about 4s. for three at Boots. What the Swedish Baptists ignored was that there are now two great factories in India making thousands of the things each day, that they are on sale in any market place at less than 1d. each and that Government family planners are giving them away as fast as they can go. The expiry date on the Baptists' sheaths is July 1971, and at the last reckoning the CMAI had almost 2 million of the original consignment left.

To avoid this sort of nonsense, Oxfam employs its Field Directors. It is they who work out how best money can be applied, and also ensure that it is properly administered when it arrives. The transfer of capital is, as we have seen, just the opening chapter of a far longer story.

Capable direction in the field must be supplemented by efficiency and expertise at home. Here Oxfam can draw on the unpaid services of its committee members, men and women who have as much experience of the developing world as a concern for its people. But the organisation has also to support a paid secretariat. And as development work becomes more complex, it will need a more specialised and perhaps larger staff. This is why, in my view, everyone's preoccupation with Oxfam's 'administrative expenses' is so trivial and irrelevant. If Oxfam spent far more money than it does to secure enough of the right administration for its projects, we should not complain. Development, as I have noted before, is not necessarily costly; but it cannot always be done on a shoestring, either.

In the opinion of Sir Denis Rickett, Vice-President of the World Bank, the amount and quality of aid given by Oxfam is now outweighed by another aspect of its work. He told a seminar, organised recently by Oxfam and the Workers' Educational Association, that the agency's greatest service was in encouraging a familiarity with the problems in development.

This is perhaps the most fundamental change that has overcome Oxfam in the sixties, and a pointer to its activities in the seventies. The organisation is no longer satisfied with a humanitarian role. Increasingly, its efforts are being directed towards revealing the causes of world poverty, and towards propagating solutions. Oxfam's educational staff supplies visual aids to schools, and seeks to have the development issue treated as a worthy – perhaps the worthiest – object of study. No course in geography nor any consideration of the historical process is considered complete by Oxfam unless it refers to development.

Oxfam can expect a financial return from this work. If children are made aware of conditions in the developing world, they may want to help improve them. Parents may even get the message. More important, it is a modest exercise in nation-building: to produce a nation not preoccupied solely with its balance of payments, but one that is committed to its wider interests and to a wider world.

The problems facing the developing world are, however, too urgent to be left to the next generation. With other voluntary agencies, Oxfam feels it must somehow foster a climate of opinion that will oblige current governments to act more forcefully. With its regional network and its familiarity with development work, it is well-placed to do so.

On a limited scale, the process has begun. Oxfam is represented on Action for World Development, a body so shamelessly propagandist that it cannot use charitable funds for all its work. It also supports the Third World First Group which is part fund-raising, part educational, and part propagandist. Individual members of Oxfam's staff are at liberty to promote reforms in the Government's aid programme, and one was a signatory of the Haslemere Declaration, the most radical exposition of the inadequacies of British aid to appear during the decade.

In Canada, where an independent Oxfam has been in action for five years, there exists more blatant encouragement to radicalise the aid issue. First the Canadian Government is less generous than our own. For each $100 of her gross national product, Canada last year sent 28 cents (·28 per cent) to developing countries; 14 of these 28 cents went in private investment, and a further seven went in surplus foodstuffs; the actual aid bill was therefore seven cents in 100 dollars (·07 per cent), and that, of course, was subject to the usual qualifications imposed by governments on their generosity.

Secondly the Canadian people are reckoned by the more resolute of their countrymen to be both less aware of and less concerned with the developing world than the British public. Visiting the Oxfam of Canada office in Toronto in June, I was told of an appeal that had been launched a few weeks earlier for the victims of the Peruvian earthquake. It stood at about $4,000. A similar fund opened in Britain after the disaster had by then passed the £100,000 mark.

Confronted by this situation, the younger members of the staff of Oxfam of Canada are utterly disenchanted with the traditional approach of the charities to development work. John Olsen, the education officer, Linda Freeman, the information officer, and Julie MacGregor, the public relations officer, sat me down one morning, and gave me a severe talking-to on the subject. And later, at lunch, Hugh Winsor, a Toronto journalist and a member of Oxfam of Canada's executive committee, delivered himself of a similar lecture.

The present educational budget of the organisation, they say, is 3 per cent of its annual income, or about £18,000. This is insufficient. If ever the Canadian people and Government are to be stirred from their supine complacency (Winsor used even stronger epithets), then more money and more time must be devoted to propaganda. Winsor favoured an immediate increase in the educational budget from 3 per cent to 25 per cent. Others would be quite happy for the time being to see the whole of Oxfam of Canada's income spent within the country.

Such suggestions are not unknown in the Oxfam office in Oxford. Here as well as in Toronto, there are arguments over policy and occasional resignations. Newspaper readers will have noted the departure of the Rev. Nicholas Stacey, deputy director of Oxfam, early in the year. And during the summer several junior members of the staff left for redder pastures.

With uncharacteristic reticence, Mr Stacey declined to help me in the preparation of this book. But he left behind at Oxford some useful jottings on his views and proposals. Like everyone else at Oxfam, Stacey knows that private aid is not enough: '. . . at the end of the day it doesn't greatly matter whether Oxfam raises £2 million or £5 million a year. What does matter is for Britain to meet the challenge of the Third World . . .' Nor would anyone take much exception to the

156

view that more educational work and political lobbying on aid could profitably be done in Britain.

Where Stacey and Oxfam parted company was over his plan to devote a quarter of Oxfam's income to these ends. It was not just the size of the sum that Oxfam's Council of Management found unacceptable, although there were doubts whether so much money could be effectively spent; it was rather that the law simply forbids charities to enter the political arena. The Charity Commissioners' report for 1969 stated: 'It is a well-established principle of charity law that a trust for the attainment of a political object is not a valid charitable trust and that any purpose with the object of influencing the legislature is a political purpose.'

Stacey's plan would have infringed this principle. He wanted the profits of Oxfam's gift shops – about £530,000 last year – and of its trading company – £98,590 last year – to pass to a new educational trust. In fact, if the trust were not considered charitable at law, only the profits of the trading company could be passed on, and then the company would face corporation tax. Even had Stacey been able to wriggle around the law, it would not have been a particularly ethical expedient. The voluntary workers who run the shops and the supporters who stock them with goods do so because they want to help Oxfam's programme overseas, not because they want to be educated by Mr Stacey.

One way of looking at the present debate within Oxfam is to take the view of the Charity Commissioners which can be paraphrased thus: Oxfam's job is to help poor people, and it should try not to think about the wider implications of its work. Another way is to take Oxfam's view of the charity laws: that they should be changed.

Leslie Kirkley, Oxfam's director, is on record as saying that the law 'is out of touch with present-day attitudes towards charity and social reform'; and Dr Leo Liepmann, whom I have quoted before, elaborated on the theme: 'We waste so much time in working out whether we can do this or whether we can do that: these grey areas must be dispelled.' He is certain that there will be a change in the charity laws during the seventies, but says that there must still be an effective way of rendering account to Oxfam's donors. 'We are the trustees of this money, and must use it for the purpose it was given. So if we want to extend our educational work, we must set up a trust which only uses money that is given for education.'

There will be another change in Oxfam's work during the seventies. In the past, the organisation has seen itself largely as a financier, leaving the administration of projects to others. In Bihar, where Oxfam is supporting a group of volunteers, we saw that image fading; in Zambia there is a similar team now at work. And the organisation hopes that many more will follow.

Apart from pleasing those friends of Oxfam around the world who have long believed that the agency has something unique to offer, this action recognises a deeper truth about development work. Money on its own is not enough. Nor should development be regarded as alms to the poor, an additional reason for discarding Oxfam's status as a 19th-century charity. It is a partnership between peoples, divided only by their past. Money can narrow the gap. Only people can bridge it.